Jesse Jackson

Titles in the People in the News series include:

PEOPLE
IN THE NEWS

Jesse Jackson

by Bradley Steffens and Dan Woog

B
J. Jackson

Lucent Books, San Diego, CA

19435-$26.60

Library of Congress Cataloging-in-Publication Data

Woog, Dan, 1953–
  Jesse Jackson / by Bradley Steffens and Dan Woog.
    p.   cm. — (People in the news)
  Includes bibliographical references and index.
  Summary: Discusses the life of Jesse Jackson, including his involvement in the civil rights movement, his presidential campaigns, and his role as freelance diplomat and world humanitarian.
  ISBN 1-56006-631-8 (lib. bdg. : alk. paper)
  1. Jackson, Jesse, 1941–   Juvenile literature. 2. Afro-Americans Biography Juvenile literature. 3. Civil rights workers—United States Biography Juvenile literature. 4. Presidential candidates—United States Biography Juvenile literature. 5. Afro-American diplomats Biography Juvenile literature. [1. Jackson, Jesse, 1941–   . 2. Civil rights workers. 3. Afro-Americans Biography.] I. Title. II. Series: People in the news (San Diego, Calif.)
E185.97.J25W66   2000
973.927'092—dc21
[B]   99–37858
                                                                      CIP

Table of Contents

Foreword

FAME AND CELEBRITY are alluring. People are drawn to those who walk in fame's spotlight, whether they are known for great accomplishments or for notorious deeds. The lives of the famous pique public interest and attract attention, perhaps because their experiences seem in some ways so different from, yet in other ways so similar to, our own.

Newspapers, magazines, and television regularly capitalize on this fascination with celebrity by running profiles of famous people. For example, television programs such as *Entertainment Tonight* devote all of their programming to stories about entertainment and entertainers. Magazines such as *People* fill their pages with stories of the private lives of famous people. Even newspapers, newsmagazines, and television news frequently delve into the lives of well-known personalities. Despite the number of articles and programs, few provide more than a superficial glimpse at their subjects.

Lucent's People in the News series offers young readers a deeper look into the lives of today's newsmakers, the influences that have shaped them, and the impact they have had in their fields of endeavor and on other people's lives. The subjects of the series hail from many disciplines and walks of life. They include authors, musicians, athletes, political leaders, entertainers, entrepreneurs, and others who have made a mark on modern life and who, in many cases, will continue to do so for years to come.

These biographies are more than factual chronicles. Each book emphasizes the contributions, accomplishments, or deeds that have brought fame or notoriety to the individual and shows how that person has influenced modern life. Authors portray their subjects in a realistic, unsentimental light. For example, Bill Gates—the cofounder and chief executive officer of the software giant Microsoft—has been instrumental in making personal computers the most vital tool of the modern age. Few dispute his business savvy, his perseverance, or his technical expertise, yet critics say he is ruthless in his dealings with competitors and driven more by his desire to maintain Microsoft's dominance in the computer industry than by an interest in furthering technology.

In these books, young readers will encounter inspiring stories about real people who achieved success despite enormous obstacles. Oprah Winfrey—the most powerful, most watched, and wealthiest woman on television today—spent the first six years of her life in the care of her grandparents while her unwed mother sought work and a better life elsewhere. Her adolescence was colored by promiscuity, pregnancy at age fourteen, rape, and sexual abuse.

Each author documents and supports his or her work with an array of primary and secondary source quotations taken from diaries, letters, speeches, and interviews. All quotes are footnoted to show readers exactly how and where biographers derive their information and provide guidance for further research. The quotations enliven the text by giving readers eyewitness views of the life and accomplishments of each person covered in the People in the News series.

In addition, each book in the series includes photographs, annotated bibliographies, timelines, and comprehensive indexes. For both the casual reader and the student researcher, the People in the News series offers insight into the lives of today's newsmakers—people who shape the way we live, work, and play in the modern age.

Introduction

The Orator

Our time has come. No grave can hold our body down. Our time has come. No lie can live forever. Our time has come. We must leave the racial battleground and come to the economic common ground and moral higher ground. America, our time has come.
—Jesse Jackson, speech before the 1984
Democratic National Convention

Some events are so important that many people can remember exactly where they were when they first heard about them or saw them happen. Often the best-remembered events are tragic: The shock of the bad news creates a memory that does not fade with time. Occasionally, however, a positive event leaves an equally strong impression. For millions of Americans, Jesse Jackson's address at the 1984 Democratic National Convention was such an event. Jackson spoke with such passion, intelligence, conviction, sincerity, and style that those who heard him were transfixed by his words. Briggette Robertson, a young black businesswoman from San Diego, California, recalled exactly where she was on the night of July 17, 1984, when Jackson spoke:

> My boyfriend—who is now my husband—and I were driving home when the speech came on the radio. It was surprising that a black man was running for president at all, but the *way* Jackson spoke and the *things* he said simply amazed us. It was thrilling. Even when we got home, we just sat in the car, listening.[1]

The Reverend Jesse Jackson waves to his supporters shortly before beginning his address to the Democratic National Convention on July 17, 1984.

The Robertsons were not the only ones mesmerized by Jackson's impassioned address. In the convention hall, the delegates listened closely. After every few sentences, they interrupted Jackson with waves of applause. In the Mississippi delegation, a white woman grasped the hand of a black colleague. Across the country, Americans began calling friends and relatives, urging them to turn on their television sets to witness the event. Although it was well past 11:00 P.M. on the East Coast, the television audience for Jackson's speech grew through the night. By the time Jackson finished, 33 million people had tuned in.

Jackson did not receive his party's nomination for president at that convention. Indeed, he has never been elected to any political office. He is a Baptist minister, but he does not lead a congregation. He has written books, but he is not known as an author. He has hosted a television program, but he is not considered a television star. He has headed several organizations, but not many people can remember their names. Everyone knows who Jesse Jackson is, but few can say what exactly he does.

Jesse Jackson delivers a speech. Jackson rose to prominence as a public speaker.

The one thing Jackson has always done is speak out. He is a professional speaker, an orator. Jackson has been speaking to the American public for almost forty years, reminding the nation of its greatness and calling on its citizens to do more to ensure that all people enjoy the same rights and privileges regardless of their race, religion, national origin, or economic standing. He is, in short, a voice of conscience.

Yet Jackson is a complex man. Although his words have made many people feel proud about themselves, they have also made others feel belittled. Jackson was a disciple of the Reverend Martin Luther King Jr., yet he has been accused of using the famed civil rights leader's death to further his own career. He formed a "Rainbow Coalition" that included blacks, poor people, Hispanics, women, and similar groups underrepresented in American politics, yet he has offended other minority groups such as Jews. He was a star football player, yet he constantly challenges young people to use their brains, not their athletic ability, to get ahead.

For more than three decades, Americans have held conflicting views of Jesse Jackson. Some people regard him as a hero. Others view him as a villain. Still others are not sure what to think. They see Jackson as a puzzle. One thing is certain: He is one of the most influential public figures of our time.

Chapter 1

Greenville, South Carolina

In 1988 JESSE JACKSON went to the Democratic National Convention in Atlanta with the second-largest number of delegates won by any Democratic candidate running for president that year. More than 7 million Americans had voted for Jackson in the 1988 Democratic primaries. Jackson's total was second only to that of former Massachusetts governor Michael Dukakis, the party's

Jesse Jackson holds aloft a young Hispanic supporter during his 1988 presidential campaign.

nominee. As the runner-up, Jackson won the opportunity to speak to the party and, via television, to the nation. Most political analysts believed that Jackson's speech was the most stirring one made by any candidate that year. In the midst of this great personal triumph, Jackson made a surprising and sobering statement. "People see me running," he said, "but they don't see what I'm running from."[2]

Jackson's wife, Jackie, who was sitting in the audience, was stunned by her husband's statement. "It was the most jolting thing, because I didn't know he would be saying that publicly," she later told a reporter.

> After that, I heard nothing else he said. Because I was thinking about South Carolina, and about Fort Pierce, Florida, and about racism and having a skin that's dark in this country, and yet here we are, pleading with you to let us make America better. I sat there, and nobody knows how hard I had to fight back tears.[3]

Jesse Jackson's candid admission revealed two important things about him. First, the pain he endured as a poor, illegitimate black child growing up in the segregated South of the 1940s and 1950s is one of the main forces that drove him to become a leader. Second, his memory of that pain is one of the main reasons why he has succeeded in becoming such a leader. When Jackson tells people who are battling hardships, "I understand," he is far more credible than many other American leaders. Because of his beginnings, Jackson felt driven to go far; and he has gone far in part because he has never forgotten his beginnings.

Illegitimate

"Jesse ain't got no daddy," the children in Greenville, South Carolina, used to call out to the young Jesse Jackson. Of course, Jackson did have a biological father, but that man, Noah Robinson, did not live with Jackson's mother, Helen Burns. Rather, he lived next door. In 1941 Noah Robinson was a married man in his thirties. Helen Burns was just sixteen years old.

A bus depot sign illustrates the American South of Jesse Jackson's youth, where strictly enforced laws kept black Americans and white Americans apart.

Early that year, the two conceived a child. Burns, a gifted singer who had earned scholarship offers from five music colleges, dropped out of Sterling High School to have the baby. Jesse Jackson later told the story this way: "Although my father's wife had three children by her previous marriage, he wanted a man-child of his own. His wife would not give him any children. So he went next door."[4]

Helen Burns gave birth to her son on October 8, 1941. She named him Jesse Louis Burns. *Jesse* was the name of Noah Robinson's father; *Louis* was Noah's middle name; *Burns* was Helen's family name. Many years later this child, who would become known to the world as Jesse Jackson, spoke about the effect that being born out of wedlock had on him. "That's why I have always been able to identify with those the rest of society labels as bastards, outcasts, and moral refuse," Jackson said. "I understand when you have no real last name. I understand. Because our genes cry out for confirmation."[5]

At first, Jesse Jackson knew nothing about his origins. "My first memory is of waking up in Mama's arms," Jackson later told a biographer, "and her showing me a picture of a group of soldiers in uniform, and pointing to one and telling me, 'This is your daddy.'"[6] The man in the picture was Charles Jackson. He had married Helen Burns on October 2, 1943. He later adopted Jesse, giving the boy the last name by which the world would come to know him.

At the end of World War II, Charles Jackson left the army and came to live with his young bride and stepson. The war veteran worked as a janitor, waiter, and hotel bellman, and he earned extra money doing odd jobs. Jesse adored his stepfather. Charles Jackson later recalled, "At four and five years old, he was calling me daddy, following me around, tugging at my knee."[7]

Outcast

Jesse Jackson's childhood idyll came to an abrupt end when Helen and Charles Jackson had a child of their own, Charles Jackson Jr. After the baby arrived, the couple sent Jesse to live with his grandmother, Matilda Burns, who lived around the corner. "Of course that hurt him," Barbara Mitchell, a friend of the family, later said, "but it was just more in all the rest of it, *so much* hurt he had to make his way through."[8]

The separation from his parents was painful for Jackson, but the move also helped strengthen his character. Matilda Burns, known as Aunt Tibby, was deeply religious and a strong believer in self-improvement. "Ain't no such word as *cain't, cain't* got drowned in a soda bottle," she told the boy. "Nothing is impossible for those who love the Lord,"[9] she added. Jackson later recalled the effect his grandmother's words had on him: "Grandmama [and] Mama always made me feel I was somebody special . . . always saying, 'You gonna be somebody. Just hold on.'"[10]

Jackson took his grandmother's can-do spirit to heart. At the age of six he got his first job, helping deliver wood in a pickup truck. When he was eight, he became the first black child to sell food at Greenville's all-white football stadium. Not all of the

The Patchwork Quilt

Of the many stories Jesse Jackson tells, this one about how a child-hood quilt helped him learn lifelong lessons is perhaps the most fa-mous. This version, which appears in Marshall Frady's *Jesse: The Life and Pilgrimage of Jesse Jackson*, was told in Iowa in 1988 during Jackson's second presidential campaign.

> One winter when I was a little boy, living in this humble little house without any heat, we couldn't afford a blanket. So my grandmother had to make us a quilt, or else we would've frozen. All we had, though, were pieces of old cloth, wool, gabardine, croker sack. But my grandmother gathered together all those patches and pieces, and when she finished sewing them to-gether, it made a big quilt that covered us and kept us warm. And that's like America. It's not a blanket made out of just one cloth. It's a great quilt made out of many patches—urban patch, rural patch, poor patch, affluent patch, black patch, white patch, different-colored patches—all held together by common threads, threads of fairness, understanding, tolerance, concern. Just like my grandmother sewed that quilt together with love and caring.

work Jackson did was for pay, however. When he was nine, he volunteered to read newspapers to illiterate adults.

A Gift for Language

Jackson attended Long Branch Baptist Church with his family every Sunday. When he was nine years old, Jackson was elected as the representative of the National Sunday School Convention in Charlotte, North Carolina. One of his duties was to report to the en-tire congregation on the group's activities. The boy did not shrink from the task. On the contrary, he relished it. At an early age Jackson had learned that he could speak in a way that held the at-tention of not only other children but adults as well. "Just as soon as he began talking, this amazing flair of phrase appeared, like some supernatural gift," recalled Julius Kilgore, one of Jackson's teachers. "If he felt it, he would express it—to anybody, white or black—with the most surprising, well, *ambitiousness* of language." [11]

Vivian Taylor, the daughter of the Reverend D. S. Sample, the minister at Long Branch, was also struck by the boy's speak-ing skills:

Jesse Jackson addresses a group of protesters outside the governor's mansion in Indianapolis, Indiana, in 1969. Throughout his life, Jackson has exhibited a gift for public speaking.

Jesse was prodigious from inception. Just the way he talked, he would seek words you never hear used by children, never heard coming from their mouths. For instance, "Pastor so-and-so *stirred* himself to *mount* the pulpit." I distinctly remember him saying that once, [he] couldn't have been more than six or seven years old. It was almost abnormal . . . how he would use words. From his very start, he was already producing these, these oratorical wonders.[12]

The young Jackson soon found he could use his gift for public speaking to earn money. When the first television sets arrived in Greenville, people who did not have their own sets, including Jackson, would drop by the homes of those who did to watch the news broadcasts. Many adults in Greenville were illiterate, so Jackson would read aloud the titles and datelines of newsreels that were shown. He announced the programs with such zeal and verve that members of the audience sometimes tipped him with pocket change. Soon, Jackson began to regularly appear at these gatherings carrying a paper cup in which to collect tips.

An Important Discovery

Sometime between the ages of six and nine, Jackson learned that Noah Robinson was his natural father. This knowledge was both a blessing and a curse. It was a blessing because Robinson was one of the most prominent members of Greenville's black community, and Jackson felt proud to be the offspring of such an important figure. It was a curse because it made Jackson feel like an outcast from his "real" family.

Noah Robinson had a good job. He graded cotton for the local textile mill, the town's largest employer. It was the highest position held by a black person in the white-owned firm. His professional standing was only one of the reasons why Robinson was well-known in the black community. He also had a reputation for standing up to white people. A part-time taxicab driver, Robinson once confronted a white cab driver for honking his horn at him for too long. The two men argued, then began to fight. Robinson, an amateur boxing champion, knocked the white man out. Another time, a white man jokingly poked Robinson in the buttocks at work. Robinson decked him, too. Instead of firing Robinson, the mill owners disciplined the white man. "It was known that I wouldn't take anything off anybody," [13] Robinson remembered.

Word of Robinson's feats spread through the black community. "I grew up hearing all these things about my father," Jackson later said. "Great boxer. Tall, upright, industrious." [14] One of Jackson's boyhood friends, Owen Perkins, said that the stories had a profound effect on his friend. "He almost worshipped Robinson," Perkins said, "completely idolized the man." [15]

Jackson became curious about his father's family. Not long after Jackson was born, the Robinson family had moved to a nice neighborhood. Jackson bicycled to his father's house and stood outside, staring at the chimney monogrammed with an iron *R*. He watched Noah junior, his half brother who was born ten months after he was, playing in the big backyard. Noah junior noticed the boy and waved. Jesse waved back, then quickly left. Noah junior had heard from a teacher that Jesse was his brother, so he asked his father if it were true. Noah senior said nothing, but Noah junior later recalled, "The expression on my father's face told me the lady was right." [16]

Noah senior did not ignore Jesse completely. Occasionally he stopped his car and watched his son play games. Sometimes he gave him money for school or clothes. Still, Noah junior observed, "Jesse loved our father, but he felt totally rejected." [17]

Segregation

The boy who grew up as an outcast from both his mother's family and his father's family soon found that he was an outcast from another family—the family of mainstream America, which was almost exclusively white. In the early 1940s a variety of laws kept black Americans and white Americans from mixing. South Carolina, a former slave state, had more segregation laws than many other states. In Greenville, blacks could not use public parks or swim in the public pool. Blacks had to sit at the back of buses, use separate rest rooms, and eat at separate lunch counters. Black children and white children attended separate schools.

Because of the tension that existed between the races, Jackson's mother taught her son not to become too friendly with whites, but the outgoing boy had a hard time accepting this advice. He made friends easily, with whites as well as blacks.

One of these friendships taught Jackson an important lesson about relations between blacks and whites. One of Jackson's white friends was the son of a grocer. When the boys would stop by the store, they would call to the boy's father to give them a free piece of candy. If he did not hear them, Jackson's friend would whistle for him. Jackson once went into the store without his friend and greeted the store owner. When the white man did not respond, Jackson whistled at him. The man grabbed his forty-five caliber pistol off the shelf, whirled around, grabbed Jackson by the arm, and held the pistol to the boy's head. He

A family pauses on November 25, 1955, to read a segregation sign posted in the railroad depot in Oklahoma City, Oklahoma.

addressed Jackson with a racial slur then warned the boy that if he ever whistled at him again, he would blow his head off.

Jackson felt he could not tell his parents about the incident. He worried that his mother would be angry at him for causing a scene, and he feared that his stepfather would attack the store owner for what he did. Looking back on the episode, Jackson says,

> What got me most was how the other people in the store, all of them black, pretended they hadn't even noticed it. *That* was really the trauma: the power of somebody

white to do whatever they wanted to a black child *right in the middle* of other blacks, and get completely away with it, not even questioned—that I never really got over, it's stayed with me to this day.[18]

The U.S. Supreme Court had ruled that segregation was legal as long as the separate public facilities for blacks and whites were equal. "Separate but equal" was the law, but only separation was enforced; equality was not. Jackson learned the true meaning of separate but equal when he started school. He later recalled,

One of my first memories is sitting on the front steps of our house on this street, waiting to go for my first day of school. I could see this school several blocks up the street with green grass and flags in front and all that—I thought that was the school Mama was talking about. So when we started walking and got to that school, I made a break for it. But Mama said, "That's not the one. You can't go there. It's another one." We kept walking. It was a school much farther away. . . . The one that didn't have any grass. They didn't plant any. Didn't mean for grass to grow here, or for children to grow either. Only place for recreation was sliding on the sand on the sidewalk along here. Books and desks, all old, battered leftovers passed down to us from the white schools.[19]

The teachers at the black schools may have been saddled with hand-me-down equipment, but they were not discouraged. In fact, they used such injustices to motivate their pupils. Jackson's sixth-grade teacher, Sara Shelton, made an especially strong impression on Jackson. He recalled that on the first day of class, Shelton started the day by writing difficult vocabulary words on the chalkboard:

We all looked around and started whispering to each other, "She got the wrong class. She thinks we the eighth-grade class." Somebody finally called out, "Uh, Mizz Shelton? Those are eighth-grade words. We only the sixth grade here." She turned around. "I know what grade you are. I work here. I know what grade I'm teaching. And you'll learn every one of these words, and a lot more like 'em 'fore this year is over. I will not teach down to you. One of you brats just might be mayor or governor or president someday, and I'm gonna make sure you're ready." And she turned back and went on writing.[20]

If Jackson absorbed these lessons inwardly, he did not show it outwardly. Shelton recalled that Jackson was not a serious student. "Like most boys, he thought school was a place to enjoy himself, to have loads of fun. . . . I noted he was a leader of devilment. If I could calm him down, the whole class would settle down." The only thing Jackson seemed serious about was football. "Sometimes he would talk to me about being a football star," Shelton remembered. "He was very ambitious in sports, but at that age he was only excellent academically when he wanted to be."[21]

The only teacher in a one-room Negro school in Veagy, Georgia, addresses her class in 1941, the year Jesse Jackson was born. Like many segregated schools, the Veagy school did not have desks for its students.

Football Scholarship

A lot of children dream about being professional athletes, but Jackson had good reason to think he had a future in athletics. By age thirteen, Jackson already stood more than six feet tall. Like most teens who grow quickly, Jackson was clumsy at first, but his coordination improved as he matured. By the time he enrolled in high school, he was an outstanding athlete. He was a star pitcher and hitter in baseball, but his favorite sport was football. The coaches quickly spotted his talent. Not only could he run and throw, but he was also a natural leader. In the 1950s, quarterbacks at all levels—from professional to high school—ran plays and also called the plays in the huddle. Sometimes they even changed the play at the line of scrimmage. Quarterbacks had to be smart, decisive, and calm under pressure. Jesse Jackson was all of these things.

As quarterback, Jackson began to earn the kind of acceptance and attention he had always sought. He heard cheers every Thursday night in the fall and had the pleasure of seeing his name appear in print in the local paper. He ran for various offices in the school and was elected to almost all of them. As his notoriety grew, Jackson also began to win more attention from Noah Robinson. Perhaps as a reaction to Robinson's growing interest in the boy, Charles Jackson legally adopted Jesse.

Unlike some teenage athletes, Jesse did not allow his success on the field to distract him from his studies. In fact, the more he succeeded as an athlete, the harder he strove to excel in school. "He was the only football player I ever had that asked for his assignment if he was going to miss class," one teacher recalled. "Jesse wanted to be known not only as a good quarterback but as a good scholar too." [22] Jackson succeeded: The one-time classroom clown graduated with the tenth-highest grade point average in his class.

Jesse was a good enough pitcher and player to be offered a small contract to play professional baseball. Likewise, his outstanding football playing earned him a college scholarship from the University of Illinois, a national football power. Jackson discussed the offers with Dan Foster, a reporter who had covered

Jackson's high school football career. Foster recalled the meeting: "I didn't think I was necessarily dealing with the guy who was going to be the best orator at two Democratic national conventions, but there was just something different, something promising about Jesse." Foster encouraged Jackson to take the scholarship. "I told him, 'Look, take the football thing'—if his pitching arm was that good, it'd still be good in four years, and if it wasn't, he'd sure as hell have him a good college education."[23] Jackson took Foster's advice.

In the fall of 1959, Jackson headed north with high hopes of escaping the racism of the South and becoming a star athlete at the University of Illinois. Neither of these dreams would come true, but they soon would be replaced by even loftier ones.

Chapter 2

The Call

W HEN JESSE JACKSON settled into his dormitory at the
University of Illinois in 1959, he had come a long way from
Greenville, South Carolina. Up to that point, Jackson's ambi-
tions had centered on himself. In a few short months, all of that
changed. Jackson became increasingly aware of a movement
sweeping across the country that promised to right many of the
wrongs he had experienced in Greenville. The goal of this
movement, known as the civil rights movement, was to ensure
that all Americans enjoyed equal rights under the law regardless
of the color of their skin. It was a movement that Jackson was
destined to join and later help lead.

In a sense, the American civil rights movement began when
the first blacks were brought to North America from Africa to
serve as slaves on white-owned land. Some blacks refused to accept their status as slaves and rebelled against their masters.
Such rebels were killed or severely beaten. Other slaves ran
away. Most of these runaway slaves died or were recaptured, but
some made their way to freedom in the northern colonies and,
later, northern states. From there, a few free blacks carried on a
crusade against the institution of slavery. The Emancipation
Proclamation of 1865 freed most of the slaves, but that did not
mean that blacks enjoyed the same rights as whites. A variety of
laws were enacted to keep blacks and whites apart.

In 1954, when Jesse Jackson was thirteen, the U.S. Supreme
Court ruled that segregation laws were unconstitutional, declar-
ing that "separate" cannot be "equal." For the first time in
American history, blacks and whites were equal under the law,
but that did not mean that the barriers to blacks would come

down on their own. Many whites planned to ignore or defy the Supreme Court's ruling. To achieve equality, blacks had to challenge the segregation laws one at a time.

One of the first protests against segregation occurred in Montgomery, Alabama, in 1955. A black minister named Martin Luther King Jr. traveled to Montgomery to challenge the

The Reverend Martin Luther King Jr., center, stands outside a courtroom in Montgomery, Alabama, in March 1956.

segregation policy of the city's bus lines. When the bus lines re-fused to comply with King's demands, the preacher organized a boycott. He urged both blacks and whites to stop riding the bus until the companies agreed to treat blacks and whites equally. For six months, bus patrons walked, bicycled, and took taxicabs instead of riding the bus. At last, the bus lines changed their poli-cies. The success of the Montgomery boycott made headlines across the country.

Like millions of other African Americans, Jesse Jackson was excited about the news from Montgomery. He and his friend Owen Perkins decided to test what would happen if they sat in the front of a bus in Greenville. They boarded a bus carrying pads and pencils to take notes in case they were harassed. The driver did nothing. Jackson and Perkins got transfer slips and repeated the process on another bus, then another. As Perkins later said,

> It was a very dangerous thing to do then, I guess. But we didn't really know how dangerous it was. We'd just chat to each other now and then, but mostly we were staring out the windows. We were seeing neighborhoods of Greenville we had never seen before. Nothing hap-pened, except we got to really know the whole town for the first time since we'd been living there.[24]

From then on, whenever Jackson rode the bus, he sat in the front. Only one driver, a man who was rumored to be a mem-ber of the Ku Klux Klan, ever challenged Jackson. The teenage boy refused to move. According to one of Jackson's teachers, Julius Kilgore, word of the showdown quickly spread through the school. "That driver was reportedly a Klansman, name something like Whitfield, and the whole black community was a little afraid of him. But it was all over the school the next day: 'Jesse stood up to Mr. Whitfield! Talked back to Mr. Whitfield!'"[25]

When Jackson left Greenville to enroll in the University of Illinois, Jackson assumed that he was leaving racial discrimination behind him. He was wrong. The first day of football practice, he and the other black freshman were separated from the other players. Jackson led the freshman team to a win over the varsity team in a scrimmage, but the coaches soon told him that he was being switched from quarterback to halfback. Jackson later said that the coach told him that "blacks could not be quarterbacks."[26] Jackson did not quit the team, but he became discouraged.

The slights continued off the field. Black athletes found leaflets in their mailboxes warning them not to socialize with white female students. When the black bandleader Count Basie gave a concert on campus, black students were not allowed to attend. Jackson was stunned:

> All that time I'd been imagining that Illinois had to be different from places down South, it wasn't at all. I wasn't prepared to handle that—I was going to the land of Lincoln, you know, the Promised Land of the North. But it was the same thing as South Carolina, just way off somewhere else.[27]

Jazz pianist and bandleader, Count Basie, performs. In 1959, Jackson and other black students were prevented from attending Basie's concert at the University of Illinois.

During his 1959 Christmas break, Jackson returned to South Carolina only to find that segregation was still intact. Jackson had a speech to prepare for a school oratory contest, so he went to the McBee Avenue Colored Branch Library to do research. He found that he needed a few more books, all of which were at the main library, which was reserved for whites only. The McBee Avenue librarian arranged for Jackson to get the books he needed, but when Jackson arrived at the main library, he was told he would have to wait six days to get them. He asked if he could look for the books himself, but the librarian said no. Frustrated, Jackson pleaded with the librarian to let him look for the books. A police officer who happened to be at the counter cut him off. "You heard what she said," the officer said. Jackson later recalled that he left by the backdoor, walked around to the front of the library, and looked up at the inscription that read "Greenville Public Library." "Tears came to my eyes," Jackson recalled. "I said to myself, 'That thing says *public*, and my father is a veteran and pays taxes. I'm going to use this library.'"[28]

Jackson cut his vacation short so he could return to the university to get the books he needed. At the university, Jackson completed the assignment and delivered the speech. Once again, Jackson's gift for public speaking shone through. He was one of three students chosen to give his speech at an annual competition. Jackson was so happy that he sent his mother a telegram to let her know about his success. At the competition, two judges gave Jackson near-perfect marks. The third, however, rated him much lower for speaking with what he termed a Negro dialect.

Despite the triumph, Jackson became disenchanted with the University of Illinois. At the end of his freshman year, Jackson decided not to return. He went home to Greenville.

Success at A&T

In the fall of 1960, Jackson enrolled in North Carolina Agricultural and Technical College (A&T), a mostly black institution in Greensboro. Several months before, four A&T students had demanded service at a department store lunch counter in

Greensboro. When they were ignored, they took out books and read. Their protest, called a sit-in, became a tactic that soon spread across the South. The Greensboro sit-in was one of the first important actions of the civil rights movement.

In July 1961 Jackson decided to make good on his pledge to integrate the main library in Greenville. He and seven other A&T students agreed to meet at the library to hold a sit-in. Before leaving for the protest, Jackson informed his mother that he would probably end up in jail. Helen Jackson told her son that she was not happy about the idea, but he went through with it anyway. As expected, the students were arrested. Reverend Hall, a local minister who had counseled the protesters, posted bail for Jackson and the others.

Charles Jackson was even more upset about Jesse's arrest than his mother was. The elder Jackson confronted his adopted son in the kitchen while the young man was making a sandwich. After asking Jesse how he was, Charles Jackson pointed out that he and Jesse's mother had worked hard to give their son everything he needed. Charles Jackson said,

> Thing is, when you go out there talkin' about you got to go to jail 'cause you can't get enough to read or eat someplace, that's sort of a reflection on me and your momma. [I] know you full of ideas about what all you think ain't right and all, but I don't want you bringing trouble around here.[29]

Jesse Jackson felt a great deal of respect for his parents, so he decided to honor their wishes. The Greenville students staged several more sit-ins that summer—at lunch counters, swimming pools, recreation parks—but Jackson did not join them. He did, however, attend the planning meetings at Reverend Hall's home. As Hall recalled,

> We would sit and talk about the theology of the movement, the philosophy of nonviolence and what Gandhi and Martin Luther King were about, and Jesus as liberator. Those were very exciting discussions . . . and Jesse

was very forthright with his suggestions. . . . He wanted awfully bad to go along with us . . . but he didn't want to be disobedient and disrespectful to his parents.[30]

At A&T Jackson became a star quarterback and honor student. He was elected student body president. He was also named president of the North Carolina Intercollegiate Council on Human Rights. As Jackson's reputation grew, the school's civil rights leaders sought to bring him into the protest movement. They approached Jackson, but he was unmoved. "They were determined to get me to be a part of the demonstrations, kept challenging me," Jackson later said, "but I expressed absolutely no interest in that business." Jackson was not as interested in symbolic actions as he was in real ones. "The point isn't sitting in, it's standing up,"[31] he explained to his fellow students with a turn of phrase that would prove to be his hallmark.

While at A&T, Jackson met someone who would eventually get him to change his mind: Jacqueline "Jackie" Lavinia Brown. The daughter of a migrant worker, she was bright and well-read.

College student Dorothy Bell is denied service at a lunch counter in downtown Birmingham, Alabama, in 1963. She and twenty other students were arrested for taking part in the lunch counter sit-in.

Like Jackson, she was a sociology major. But her first impression of Jackson was not good. In fact, she found him "impatient, audacious and loud."[32] Eventually, however, she realized that she and Jackson had something in common:

> We felt we were at A&T to obtain something much greater than the small towns and communities we'd left, to make a difference in the world. And then to bring that big something back to those communities, to create a new community. That's what we agreed on. We were very serious young people.[33]

Jackson and Brown spent countless hours talking about the issues of the day. Brown's ideas were more radical than Jackson's. She thought Fidel Castro, the Communist leader of Cuba, represented "the new world order," and she wrote a paper explaining why Communist China should be allowed into the United Nations. Jackson was dismayed. "Fidel Castro? Communist?" Brown remembers Jackson warning her, "You shouldn't go around talking like this, you may get in trouble."[34] Although Brown disagreed with him, she appreciated his concern for her well-being. At the same time, Brown's strong opinions and zestful personality spurred Jackson to become bolder in his own thinking.

The two A&T students began to spend all of their free time together, and Brown eventually became pregnant by Jackson. Remembering the pain of being known as a bastard, Jackson wanted to make sure that his own child suffered no such disgrace. He quickly proposed to Brown, and she accepted. The wedding took place on New Year's Eve 1962, in Jackson's parents' home in Greenville. The ceremony was conducted by Reverend D. S. Sample, the preacher whose sermons had inspired Jackson since he was ten.

Civil rights protests were sweeping the South as the newlyweds prepared for the birth of their child. Jackson was drawn toward the movement. His professors, including Samuel Proctor, taught him about Mohandas Gandhi and Martin Luther King Jr.'s vision of nonviolent protest. Jackson was greatly impressed

A Common Goal

In a television interview for the PBS show *Frontline*, "The Pilgrimage of Jesse Jackson," Jackson's wife, Jackie, explains the idealism she shares with her husband.

> We were given an opportunity to make a difference in the world. We were basically raised unselfishly. We are to bring things back to the community, or create a new community. That was our responsibility and obligation when we left home. To bring something big back. Something new, and you're to be a better person when you return.
>
> And it doesn't mean physically returned. You're supposed to change and make things better for other people, those who are back home. How could we do that? We had to join with people and forces who were making a change.
>
> So Jesse and I saw this as our obligation when we went to A&T. We couldn't disappoint the people back home by returning as dependent on society or them. We had to go out and make a difference. So we thought alike. . . . We were very serious young people, very directed, very goal-oriented and very responsible for not only our families, but for our country. We were— are—a part of a bigger thought and idea and society.

Jacqueline and Jesse Jackson.

by Proctor, who had been a student with King at Boston University and who believed, like King, that peaceful protest could bring about significant change. Jackson joined thousands of people in a mass march on Washington, D.C., in August 1963, where he heard King deliver the speech for which he is best known. In that speech, King proclaimed, "I have a dream." Jackson, like millions of others, was deeply moved by King's words.

Back in Greensboro, Jackson attended a meeting of the local chapter of the Congress of Racial Equality (CORE). After the meeting, CORE leaders met to discuss whether to ask Jackson about becoming more active in the movement. The campus chaplain, A. Knighton Stanley, later recalled that the fear among the group was that Jackson, who was already known as a strong leader, would take over the leadership of the group. "There was also some feeling that he hadn't paid his dues, so why should he lead?"[35] Stanley said. Others believed that Jackson would be an asset to the group. The members voted to have Stanley ask Jackson to join. Jackson agreed.

Soon after joining CORE, Jackson faced one of the most difficult and momentous decisions of his life. CORE had planned a march on downtown Greensboro. On the morning of the march, an A&T administrator named L. C. Dowdy met with the leaders of the march. He explained that members of the state legislature had warned him that if A&T students took part in more protests, the state government might take away the

The Reverend Martin Luther King Jr. greets the crowd assembled to hear him speak in Washington, D.C., in August 1963.

school's accreditation. If that happened, the school's diplomas would be worthless and the students would have wasted their academic careers. Dowdy left the decision of whether to march up to the students. Thirteen hundred students had gathered outside a church to begin the march, but the leaders were still debating what to do. Jackson and the others went out onto the porch of the church to speak to the crowd. Jackson did not want to lose his diploma, but he recalled the words of Jesus in the Garden of Gethsemane. "It was 'Not my will, but thine be done,'" Jackson remembered. "My will was to go back to the campus. But I couldn't, 'cause I knew, just as a quarterback, you can never choose the path of having no confidence." Finally, it was Jackson's turn to speak. He looked out over the crowd and, despite his misgivings, he knew what to say. "History is upon us," he told the crowd. "This generation's judgement is upon us. Demonstrations without hesitation! Jail without bail! Let's go forward!" [36]

As the CORE demonstrations continued, Jackson gave speeches designed to keep everyone's spirits up. After one of these speeches in May 1963, the campus chaplain compared Jackson's speaking abilities to those of King.

With a baby on the way and graduation approaching, Jackson realized that he soon had to decide what to do with his life. He wanted to be an agent for change in America, but he was not sure how to do it. One way could be through a career in law. The famous black attorney Thurgood Marshall had recently been appointed to the U.S. Supreme Court, inspiring Jackson to think seriously about becoming a lawyer.

Another way to bring about change could be through the ministry. King, the leader of the civil rights movement, was a minister. Ministers often were the most prominent members of the black community. As a boy, Jackson had daydreamed about being a minister as he listened to the sermons of Reverend Sample and other preachers. "I'd sit there watching them, but all I was really seeing was myself up there in that pulpit," Jackson later said. When he was fifteen, Jackson told his friend Owen Perkins, "I want to be a minister. That's what I'm gonna be." [37]

A Great Speech

A. Knighton Stanley, a member of the campus ministry at North Carolina A&T, was interviewed for the PBS television show *Frontline*, "The Pilgrimage of Jesse Jackson." He remembered an impromptu speech Jackson gave in 1963 when the civil rights movement in Greensboro was growing. Even then, Jackson's oratorical gifts were evident.

> It was a marvelous speech. Extremely articulate. Extremely knowledgeable. He was on point every step of the way in this speech. It flowed. It was poetic. And it was a marvelous thing. Martin Luther King's letter from the Birmingham jail had come out a little while before Jesse gave that speech. And those of us who heard it, and we had heard some great speakers in the movement, we said, "My God, this speech that Jesse has given is comparable to Martin Luther King's letter from the Birmingham jail."
>
> And so after the little rally, the gathering was over, we rushed to Jackson and we said, "Jesse, this is a marvelous speech and we got to get with you now so we can record it and write it down because this is the kind of speech that you want to publish and keep." And Jesse looked at us and he was quite surprised and said, "What did I say?" He had no sense of the impact of that speech, the wisdom of it.

In college, however, Jackson began to doubt if the ministry was really right for him. Most preachers he had known were more concerned with preparing souls for heaven than with righting wrongs on earth—the opposite of how Jackson felt. Jackson increasingly felt drawn to a career in law, but that suddenly changed. Charles Carter, Jackson's roommate at A&T, remembered the event: "One night he woke up and said he had had an odd dream. He said he thought he had been called to preach. He was shaking. I never saw him look so serious before." [38]

Jackson was so moved by the experience that he called Noah Robinson in Greenville to discuss it. "Jesse told me he dreamed he would lead an army across the waters like Moses did," Robinson recalled. Robinson was struck by the fact that Jackson was then the same age that his own father had been when he had decided to become a minister. "I remember telling him I don't know if you could really lead an army, but you might be a good preacher like your granddaddy was." [39]

Jackson was not sure that his dream qualified as a pastoral call. He met with Samuel Proctor to discuss the matter. "I thought the call would be some cataclysmic religious experience like waking up some night and falling off a horse like Paul, or cutting flips in the air, shouting or something,"[40] Jackson later said. Proctor told the younger man that the call to the ministry was not always dramatic. Sometimes it was a gradual realization of a service to be performed or a role to be played.

Proctor told Jackson that seminary school involved everything Jackson liked: poetry, history, sociology, and philosophy. Jackson was still unsure. He explained that he was more interested in changing society than in saving souls. Proctor told him, "You don't have to enter the ministry because you want to save people from a burning hell. It may be because you want to see his kingdom come on earth as it is in heaven."[41]

Although he was still unsure about what to do, Jackson applied for and received a grant from the Rockefeller Fund for Theological Education. The grant, Reverend Stanley recalled, was for "a trial year for a person who hadn't fully decided for the ministry yet, which was appropriate for Jesse, because there were still some uncertainties there."[42]

Jackson was just one of twenty-five black students in the United States and Canada to receive the Rockefeller Fund grant. In September 1964 he enrolled in the Chicago Theological Seminary. "I decided to go to the seminary," he later said, "to learn how to do without the law to change society, change it in deeper ways."[43]

Within a few short years, Jackson would do just that.

Chapter 3

The Martin Luther King Jr. Years

JESSE JACKSON CHOSE to attend the Chicago Theological Seminary in part because he wanted to emulate Martin Luther King Jr. Ironically, Jackson eventually left the seminary because of King as well. Jackson was destined to become not only a follower of King but also one of his closest aides. The relationship between the two men would have far-reaching consequences for them as well as for the civil rights movement and the nation.

After the tumult of the Greensboro demonstrations, Jesse Jackson returned to Illinois hoping to lead a quiet life of contemplation. Jackie Jackson was pregnant with their second child as the two settled into a modest apartment in Chicago. Jackson knew he had to find work and find it quickly if he and his family were to survive in the city.

Through his church, Jackson met the mother of John Johnson, the founder of *Jet* and *Ebony* magazines, two of the leading black publications in the country. Johnson's mother asked her son to give Jackson a job. Johnson hired Jackson to sell the magazines to newsstand dealers. As Jackson traveled throughout the city, he learned about the poverty, unemployment, and poor housing conditions in Chicago's inner-city neighborhoods. He was struck once more by what he had learned as a student at the University of Illinois: The problems faced by blacks in the North were different than those faced by blacks in the South, but they were just as severe.

Early in 1965 Jackie Jackson returned to Greenville to give birth to her and Jesse's second child. Meanwhile, Jesse Jackson continued to lead the sedate life of a seminary student. All that changed on March 7, 1965. This time it was not a dream that suddenly changed Jackson's life but a kind of nightmare.

Watching the late news in the lounge of his apartment building, Jackson saw footage of a civil rights demonstration led by King in Selma, Alabama. Other civil rights demonstrations had been met with violence, but nothing like what was happening Selma. White state troopers waded into the crowd on horseback, clubbing the demonstrators with nightsticks. People crumpled under the blows; blood flowed. A few onlookers hurled rocks and bottles at the crowd. Watching the scenes on television, Jackson was outraged.

He hardly slept that night. The next morning, he walked into the student cafeteria, jumped up on a table, and began to speak. He explained to the astonished students what was happening in Selma. He described the situation as a moral challenge and called for volunteers to travel with him to Selma to show support for the demonstrators. Twenty seminary students—all

Injured civil rights protesters are helped away from the demonstration in Selma, Alabama, in March 1965. Outraged by the bloodshed, Jesse Jackson led a band of protesters from Chicago to Selma to take part in the demonstration.

white—and several faculty members packed their bags and left with Jackson for Selma.

After driving eighteen hours, Jackson and his band of protesters arrived in Selma. Thousands of people—black and white—were milling about in the streets. Most of the demonstrators were excited to be there but were not quite sure what to do next. Jesse Jackson, however, knew exactly what he wanted to do. He immediately sought out the leaders of the demonstration.

An all-night vigil was taking place outside a church known as Brown Chapel. Jackson approached one of the leaders of the vigil, Andrew Young, an aide to King who later became the U.S. ambassador to the United Nations and the mayor of Atlanta, Georgia. "Jesse came up, this big, handsome, natural leader of a young man," Young later recalled, "not just as somebody wanting to take part but as the leader of the Chicago delegation, saying 'What do you want *my people* to do?'"[44]

Jackson also sought out Ralph Abernathy, King's chief assistant. Jackson asked what he could do to help keep the vigil going. Abernathy thanked Jackson for his interest but did not give him anything specific to do. Before the two parted company, Jackson asked Abernathy for a job with King's organization, the Southern Christian Leadership Conference (SCLC).

The next day Jackson continued to look for ways to help with the demonstration. "He immediately got to the front, automatically started directing marchers, functioning, wholly unbidden, as a staff member," Andrew Young recalled. At one point, Jackson took to the steps of Brown Chapel and began to give an impromptu speech. King's aides were dismayed. "I got a little annoyed because he was giving orders from the steps of Brown Chapel and nobody really knew who he was,"[45] said Young.

King's followers were a close-knit group, and many resented the way the newcomer thrust himself into the action. Others, however, admired him. "People criticized Jesse for being forward and aggressive, but in fact that was exactly the kind of self-assurance and assertiveness we needed,"[46] Young later conceded. Abernathy was one of those most impressed by the brash young man, and he arranged for Jackson to meet with King.

Ralph Abernathy, chief assistant to Martin Luther King Jr., greets a supporter. Impressed by Jesse Jackson's enthusiasm, Abernathy arranged a meeting between Jackson and King.

The meeting in Selma in 1965 was not the first time Jackson came face-to-face with King. The two had met briefly at an airport once before. This time, however, they spoke in some depth about the civil rights movement. Jackson boldly told King to take the civil rights movement north, where Jackson could help. Although King was impressed with Jackson's energy and dedication, he did not respond at the time to Jackson's proposal.

King and his followers planned to march from Selma to Montgomery, Alabama. The day that Jackson met with King, however, the marchers only got as far as a nearby bridge, where they again were stopped by mounted troopers. King had worked out an agreement with a mediator to stop the march at the bridge that day, so there was no violence.

After the brief, peaceful march, Jesse Jackson became ill and decided to return to Chicago. On the way home, Jackson stopped and made a phone call to find out how his wife was doing. He learned that Jackie had given birth to a baby boy, Jesse junior.

One week later, King led thirty thousand protesters on a triumphant march from Selma to Montgomery. Although Jackson watched the march from afar, he felt part of the historic event. When Jackie returned to Chicago with their son, Jesse told her all about the two days in Selma. She later recalled, "It changed his life. All he wanted to do now was work closely with Dr. King." [47]

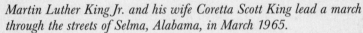

Martin Luther King Jr. and his wife Coretta Scott King lead a march through the streets of Selma, Alabama, in March 1965.

The Youngest Aide

Six months after Selma, Jackson was given a part-time job with the SCLC. Just twenty-four years old, Jackson was the youngest of King's aides. He was assigned to Operation Breadbasket, a program aimed at getting major companies to hire more black workers. Jackson knew a lot about public speaking and protests, but he did not know much about business. Still, he learned quickly. His first success came when he convinced a dairy to add or upgrade 44 positions for African Americans. Next came a grocery chain. They hired 183 black men and women, most as laborers but some at the management level.

Inspired by those successes, Jackson began negotiating with A&P, a national supermarket chain. It agreed to add nearly one thousand jobs for black people. Those A&P jobs provided an additional $22 million in income for residents of Chicago's impoverished South Side.

By 1967 Operation Breadbasket was a nationwide program. As one of its most experienced organizers, Jesse Jackson traveled

Jesse Jackson gives a clenched-fist salute from the back of a police van after he and other members of Operation Breadbasket were arrested during a sit-in.

around the country sharing his knowledge. He negotiated with businesspeople, taught civil rights leaders how to organize Operation Breadbasket in their own cities, and encouraged local residents to put pressure on companies to hire African Americans.

The travel and responsibility took a toll on Jackson's studies. A fellow student recalled, "It was difficult for him to stay focused on the academic discipline of reading the books and writing the papers and getting the job done in the classroom. He was always more eager to get on with the work at hand out there in the world."[48] Because of the time constraints he faced, Jackson asked for special favors from his professors. In one class, he asked to give a speech rather than write a paper. He also refused to write out his sermons for a class in preaching. As a result, Jackson received a D in the course.

The faculty was divided over Jackson. One of his professors found him to be "an electrifying chap." Another, however, said he had "spectacular gall."[49] Some professors admired Jackson for his involvement with the civil rights movement. Others felt he should withdraw from the seminary because of his inattention to his studies.

Six months before graduation, Jackson decided to leave the Chicago Theological Seminary and work full-time for King. According to Jackson, King told him, "Come on with me full time, and you'll learn more theology in six months than you would in six years at the seminary."[50]

King and Jackson

Jackson spent just two and a half years with King. At the time, the civil rights movement was at its peak. In small southern towns and large northern cities, millions of Americans were marching, sitting in, and fighting for the rights of black people. Civil rights was the topic of intense congressional debates, and President Lyndon Johnson made it the centerpiece of his "Great Society" plan. A number of black spokesmen emerged, but the undisputed national leader was Martin Luther King Jr. And Jesse Jackson was working for him.

When Jackson had approached King in Selma with the idea of taking the civil rights struggle to the North, he did not know that King and other members of the SCLC had been discussing the same idea for several months. In the summer of 1966, King at last came to Chicago. For months, Jackson had worked to make the visit a success. He helped organize rallies for King that drew more than sixty thousand people.

The campaign in the North was different from the campaign in the South. In the North, segregation was the result of economics, not laws. Blacks and whites were separated by a vast gap in income. Rich whites did not have to pass laws to keep blacks out of their neighborhoods. The price of homes did that for them. In the cases when blacks could afford homes in white areas, white-managed banks often denied home loans to families because they were black. The gap in income affected not only housing but other areas as well—education, employment, and politics among them.

To address issues in the North, King had to broaden the scope of his message. He had to delve into areas of behavior that many whites did not want to hear about. Most northern whites were quick to condemn segregation laws of the South, but they were slower to admit that the structure of society in the North also denied basic rights to blacks. As a result, King lost a great deal of his support among whites. He lost even more when urban riots broke out in black areas of Los Angeles and several northern cities. It seemed to many whites that the civil rights movement was out of control.

Poor People's Campaign

King also began to lose support in the black community. As he broadened his focus, King saw that African Americans were not the only people to suffer from poverty. In the summer of 1967 King proposed a national "Poor People's Campaign" that would include Hispanics, Indians, and poor white Americans.

Some of King's aides, including Jackson, were uneasy with this shift in focus. They thought that King should keep his attention on African Americans. But while most of King's aides

A Hard Act to Follow

Bob Lucas, a civil rights activist in Chicago in the 1960s, was interviewed for the television program *Frontline,* "The Pilgrimage of Jesse Jackson." He recalled the time Jesse Jackson upstaged Martin Luther King Jr. at a rally.

> On this Sunday I was the moderator, and there were three speakers: Jesse Jackson, Dr. King and James Farmer. And Farmer spoke first because he had to leave, and after Farmer spoke, I brought Jesse on. And Jesse Jackson gave this rousing speech—a really great speech. I had never heard Jesse speak before, neither had most of the people in this church and he literally brought the house down and he brought people to their feet six or seven times while he was speaking and you know people really enjoyed it, and I'm certain a lot of people were saying to him, "Hey, this guy is gonna be great, we may have another King here this afternoon."
>
> And when Jesse finished, Dr. King called me and I went over and he says, "Bob, I think that I have laryngitis and I'm not going to be able to speak today and will you please tell your people." Well, I don't believe that Dr. King had developed laryngitis. I believed that Doc didn't think that he was equal to Jesse that day, you know. As you know public speakers, some days your arm is sound like a baseball pitcher. Some days you feel up to it, and some days you aren't, and I think that Dr. King was somewhat demoralized as a result of Jesse's great speech and again, he decided that he wasn't really up to it, he couldn't equal it and decided not to speak.

voiced their concerns in private, Jackson spoke out in public. King's aides did not know what to make of him. They had been taught to work quietly in the background. When Jackson expressed his own ideas on television or was quoted in newspapers, King's aides became upset. Besieged on all sides, King began to lose patience with Jackson as well.

King and Memphis

In the spring of 1968, King's frustration with Jackson began to show. King and Abernathy had traveled to Memphis, Tennessee, to lead a march in support of the sanitation workers who were on strike. To King's dismay, the march quickly turned into a riot. Afterward, King blamed himself for the botched protest. He returned to SCLC headquarters in Atlanta and called a meeting to decide what to do about the sanitation strike. Jackson attended the meeting and spoke out against supporting the sanitation strike any further, arguing that the issue was too small for King. Jackson urged his mentor to remain focused on the Poor People's Campaign and encouraged him to return to Chicago.

King became frustrated with the naysayers in the group. He knew that he had achieved some of his greatest successes by supporting small causes and he felt that the sanitation strike was deserving of his attention. Finally, King told the group, "I can't take all this on by myself. I need you to take your share of the load."[51] With that, the leader of the SCLC stormed out of the room.

Jackson and Young followed after King, and Jackson called to him, "Doc? Doc? Don't worry, everything's going to be all right." It was the wrong thing to do. King stopped in his tracks, turned toward Jackson, and, pointing at the younger man for emphasis, shot back,

> Jesse, everything's not going to be all right. If things keep going the way they're going now, it's not SCLC but the whole country that's in trouble. . . . If you're so interested in doing your own thing, that you can't do what this organization is structured to do, if you want to carve out your own niche in society, go ahead. But for God's sake, don't bother me![52]

Jackson was shocked. He returned to Chicago without speaking to King again.

A few days later, King had second thoughts about what he had said to Jackson. He phoned Jackson to more calmly make his point. King explained that the SCLC was one of the few hopes the nation had to heal the wounds of racism, but that for the group to succeed, everyone had to work together. He asked Jackson to join him in Memphis, explaining that the goal there was quite similar to the economic work Jackson was doing. Jackson agreed to rejoin his mentor.

On April 3, 1968, King delivered a powerful speech at the Masonic Temple in Memphis. Later, Jackson called Jackie to tell her about the event. Jackie Jackson recalled, "He called me . . . and told me that Martin had given the most brilliant speech of his life. That he was lifted up and had some mysterious aura around him, and a power as if saying that now everything's going to be all right."[53]

The next day, while standing on the balcony of the Lorraine Motel where he was staying, King invited Jackson to join him and a few others for dinner at the home of a local preacher, Reverend Samuel Kyle. Reverend Kyle then informed King that "Jesse was the instigator of this thing. He already got himself invited."[54] King laughed at his young aide's behind-the-scenes maneuver. The turmoil between the two men had clearly passed.

From left, Hosea Williams, Jesse Jackson, Martin Luther King Jr., and Ralph Abernathy stand on the balcony of the Lorraine Motel in Memphis, Tennessee, the day before King was assassinated.

Jackson then informed King that he had brought along a member of his Operation Breadbasket band, Ben Branch, to perform at that night's meeting. King called down to the singer, "Ben, I want you to sing 'Precious Lord' for me tonight like you never sung it before. Want you to sing it real pretty." [55]

A moment later, as King turned to go back into his room for his topcoat, a single rifle shot rang out. The bullet struck King in the neck, driving him backward into the wall and causing him to fling his arms outward. Then the great civil rights leader slumped to the floor. Jackson and the others rushed to King's side, but there was nothing they could do. Within minutes King was dead, and Jesse Jackson's life had changed forever.

Chapter 4

"I Am Somebody"

T HE DEATH OF Martin Luther King Jr. left a void in the civil rights movement. Despite the setbacks he endured in the final years of his life, King was still the most renowned and respected black American in history. No one person could or would take his place. Nevertheless, someone had to fill the vacuum. Someone had to lead. That person was Jesse Jackson.

The Stain of Blood

How Jackson went about filling the void left by the slain civil rights leader created a controversy that has lasted for decades.

The controversy began at the Lorraine Motel in the aftermath of King's assassination. After King's body was taken to the hospital, Jesse Jackson called King's wife, Coretta, in Atlanta to tell her King had been shot. After the phone call, King's aides held a hurried meeting. They all knew King was dead, but they agreed that no one would talk to the press until they had more information about King's injuries.

Jackson went outside, looking for a ride to the hospital morgue where King had been taken. Reporters who had raced to the scene of the assassination besieged Jackson with questions. Jackson knew that millions of people around the world at that moment were waiting, hoping, and praying for some word about the fallen leader. Despite his agreement with the other SCLC leaders, Jackson spoke to the reporters:

> The black people's leader, our Moses, the once-in-a-400- or 500-year leader, has been taken from us by hatred and bitterness. Even as I stand at this hour, I cannot even

allow hate to enter my heart at this time, for it was sick-
ness, not meanness, that killed him. People were . . . in
pandemonium, some were in shock, some were crying,
hollering, "Oh, God!" And I immediately started running upstairs to where he was and I caught his head and
I tried to feel his head and I asked him, I said, "Dr. King,
do you hear me? Dr. King, do you hear me?" And he
didn't say anything and I tried to hold his head. And by
that time. . . .[56]

Jackson broke off in midsentence. He and other King aides
hurried to the morgue to view their fallen leader, then quickly
left. Jackson called Jackie at home in Chicago. "Jackie, Dr. King
has been shot," he told his wife. "He is dead. There's a lot going
on down here, I don't understand any of it."[57] He told Jackie that
he was coming home immediately.

As word spread about King's murder, thousands of African
Americans became enraged. Riots broke out in several cities. By
the time Jackson landed in Chicago, the city was ablaze.
Chicago was not the only city to suffer riots, but it was one of the
worst hit. Looters and arsonists caused $10-million worth of
property damage. In response, Chicago's mayor Richard Daley
ordered his police officers to shoot anyone seen carrying a
weapon.

When Jackie Jackson met her husband at the airport, she noticed that his shirt was stained with blood. On the drive home,
Jesse Jackson hardly spoke. Once home, he got into bed without
undressing or even taking off his shoes. Jackie remembers telling
her husband that he should take off the bloody shirt. "He told
me, 'I'll never take this shirt off. This is Martin's blood.'"[58]

Controversial Speeches

The next morning Jackson appeared on NBC's *Today* show, still
wearing the blood-stained shirt. Jackson invoked the name of
Martin Luther King Jr. and pleaded for an end to the riots. He
explained that the blood on his shirt came from the fallen civil
rights leader:

A store burns during a riot that followed the assassination of Martin Luther King Jr. During the riots, Jesse Jackson appeared on television and appealed for calm.

I come here with a heavy heart because on my chest is the stain of blood from Dr. King's head. . . . This blood is on the chest and hands of those who would not have welcomed him here yesterday. . . . He went through, literally, a crucifixion. I was there. And I'll be there for the resurrection.[59]

In other statements to the press, Jackson implied that he had actually held the dying King in his arms.

Jackson's version of the events was disputed by several of King's aides. Hosea Williams, the director of the SCLC's voter registration project, said, "The only person who cradled Dr. King was [Ralph] Abernathy."[60] Some of King's aides believed that Jackson was trying to advance his own career by suggesting that he was the closest person to King when he died. Don Rose, an SCLC adviser, is one of those who accused Jackson of using King's blood for selfish reasons. "He was thinking very clearly, thinking ahead, thinking of, frankly, his own career, the future of the movement and his role within it,"[61] said Rose.

Williams also criticized Jackson's statements. "It's a helluva thing to capitalize on a man's death, especially one you professed to love,"[62] he said. Coretta Scott King, Martin Luther King Jr.'s widow, was so upset by accounts of Jackson's actions that for many years she refused to speak to him.

Others were not so quick to condemn Jackson's behavior. They believed his intent was to show that the civil rights movement was still strong, that the cause would not die because its leader had fallen. Jackie Jackson later reflected, "We could not let the enemies of peace and the enemies of our movement win like that."[63]

As a student of history and religion, Jackson understood the power of symbols. For example, when President John F. Kennedy was killed in Dallas, Texas, in 1963, Lyndon Johnson took the oath of office aboard *Air Force One* on the flight back to Washington. According to the Constitution, Johnson was already president, but taking the oath had symbolic power. Similarly, when a king or queen dies, his or her crown is placed on the head of the successor to show that the monarchy lives on. In the Bible, the prophet Elijah gave his follower, Elisha, his mantle as a sign that God would continue to work miracles on earth even after Elijah was gone.

Whether by design or impulse, Jackson used his shirt as a symbol. The blood-stained garment conveyed in ways that words never could that, while Martin Luther King was dead, his closest followers—and the movement he led—were very much alive.

Coretta Scott King and her daughter Bernice arrive in Memphis, Tennessee, the day after Martin Luther King Jr. was murdered.

Because of the bitterness surrounding his actions, Jesse Jackson no longer comments about the statements he made after King's death. In 1988 he told the *Washington Post*, "I *never* respond to (questions about) it. It has no useful or redeeming value. To whom does it matter, the continuous rehearsal of that?" [64]

The Movement Goes On

The controversy over Jackson's actions was overshadowed by the more pressing issue of who would lead the civil rights movement. Many people thought that person should be Jackson. On the Saturday after King was shot, Jackson spoke at a weekly meeting sponsored by Chicago's Operation Breadbasket. The week before, Jackson had drawn a crowd of four hundred people. After King's death, four thousand people showed up to hear what he had to say. Jackson sensed that the yearning for leadership was not confined to Chicago. He arranged to speak on as many television shows and radio programs as he could. Everywhere his message was the same: Much work remained to be done.

Resurrection City

The leaders of the SCLC decided that the group's work would continue in the nation's capital, Washington, D.C. Before King's death, the group had discussed holding a demonstration for the Poor People's Campaign on the Mall, located between the Lincoln Memorial and the Capitol. The idea was to summon poor people from across America to Washington to show lawmakers, the media, and tourists that the problems of poverty

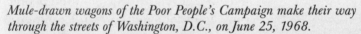
Mule-drawn wagons of the Poor People's Campaign make their way through the streets of Washington, D.C., on June 25, 1968.

affected Americans of every race, religion, and ethnic background. The demonstrators would build an encampment as a re-
minder that poor people could build lives for themselves. The
name of the encampment was to be "Resurrection City."

Ralph Abernathy, who replaced King as the leader of the
SCLC, decided to go ahead with the plans as a tribute to the
undying spirit of Martin Luther King Jr. Abernathy appointed
Jackson as the "mayor" of Resurrection City. As mayor, Jackson
was responsible for organizing marches, giving speeches, and
focusing media attention on the issue of poverty in America.

The grand plans for Resurrection City were never realized.
After a few days filled with energy and high hopes, spirits
sagged. Two thousand people crammed into fifty plywood shel-
ters covered with plastic. Days of rain turned Resurrection City
into a sea of mud. Soon there was drinking, fighting, and theft.
Morale was low. Disappointed with how the event was unfold-
ing, Abernathy replaced Jackson as mayor of Resurrection City
with Hosea Williams.

Despite the affront, Jackson did not go home. He continued to
take part in the rally. Jackson led a group of three hundred people
inside a hearing of the House Interstate and Foreign Commerce
Committee. Speaking through a bullhorn, he told lawmakers,

> We have been the nation's laborers, its waiters. Our
> women have raised its presidents on their knees. We
> have built the highways. We have died in wartime fight-
> ing people we were not even mad at. America worked
> for 350 years without paying us. Now we deserve a job
> or an income.[65]

In the midst of the two-month encampment, Jackson became ill with hepatitis and ptomaine poisoning. Despite his
weakened condition, he spoke to the crowd from the back of a
flatbed truck. Later, he recalled what would be known for years
as his greatest address:

> It was a rainy morning, and our heads were hanging low,
> our hearts were heavy. When I looked down from the
> back of that truck, it was mostly women and children, all

colors, a rainbow of them. And they looked up at me for something I could not give them—I couldn't give them any money for a bus ticket back home, nor could I take away the pain in their hearts because Dr. King had been killed. But then I remembered something. That when you've lost everything—every *thing*—you still have your humanity and your integrity, you still have your will to be somebody. So I asked all of them standing down there before me, asked them to repeat these words, *I am somebody.* It just came out of me—"I am somebody." And they came back, *I am somebody!* I went on, they answering back each line, "I may be poor, but I *am . . . somebody.* . . . Red, yellow, brown, black and white . . . we are *all* precious in God's sight." I could see pride and hope come back into their faces. "Respect me! . . . Never neglect me! . . . For I *am . . . somebody!*" It was like, as I went along, the words just formed in front of me, and it began to transform that whole morning.[66]

The man who as a boy had been taunted as a nobody was encouraging others to respect themselves and demand respect from others. King had used the words *I am somebody* as the refrain of a speech in 1964, but that morning in Washington, "I am somebody!" became Jesse Jackson's signature phrase.

National Notice

After two months, the permit that allowed the construction of Resurrection City expired, and members of the National Guard moved in to tear down the ramshackle village. Tired, disillusioned, and hungry, two thousand poor people went home. Resurrection City had not lived up to the hopes of its organizers, but it had made Jesse Jackson a national celebrity. The *New York Times* hailed Jackson as "probably the most persuasive black leader on the national scene." *Life* magazine called him perhaps "the most astute black political leader"[67] in America. In a 1970 poll of admired black figures, Jackson ranked ninth, right after Supreme Court justice Thurgood Marshall and ahead of Massachusetts senator Edward Brooke and heavyweight champion Muhammad Ali.

Jesse Jackson addresses a rally at the Harvard Law School in Cambridge, Massachusetts, in 1990.

Jackson looked the part of a leader. At 6 feet 2 inches and 220 pounds, he commanded attention in a crowd. Mabel Walker, an early supporter, recalled that he had "gray eyes— light eyes . . . *piercing* eyes. . . . He put his arms out, he had on a robe or dashiki or something, and he looked to me just like Jesus." [68] His physical presence was imposing, but his personality was even more impressive. "He had an articulate kind of self-confidence intellectually," Andrew Young once explained. "And there was a zeal. There was a determination to make the world a better place. And . . . he was willing to commit himself to the struggle with few, if any, reservations." [69]

As a speaker, Jackson knew how to reach out and inspire his audience. Writer Eddie Stone noted that Jackson would never settle for boredom when he can say something that will create controversy. Using speech patterns that range from Harvard educated to Southern field worker, Jackson will shift and modulate according to his message. He will retreat into humble sensitivity, then strike back with the voice of a forceful revolutionary.[70]

After Resurrection City, Jackson was named national director of Operation Breadbasket, the program he had successfully run in Chicago for years. His job was to convince companies to hire more black workers, use more black-owned firms for services ranging from trash removal to construction, and take black consumers more seriously. By 1974 Chicago had six black-owned banks and was considered a model for black business. Politicians came from as far as Africa to study Operation Breadbasket.

But Jackson did more than run an economic project. With his ability to speak clearly and forcefully on a wide range of issues, Jackson became something of a celebrity.

The Break with the SCLC

Despite his fame, or perhaps because of it, a rift developed between Jackson and the SCLC. It occurred over a program known as Black Expo. The first Black Expo was organized by Jackson and the SCLC in Chicago in 1970. Part business fair, part educational exhibit, and part carnival, the exposition was a huge success. More than five hundred companies and thousands of visitors attended. The next year Jackson organized a Black Expo on his own, without telling the SCLC. Ralph Abernathy was furious. He suspended Jackson for sixty days.

Jackson promptly resigned from the SCLC. On Christmas morning 1971, Jackson introduced a new organization: Operation PUSH, or People United to Save Humanity. Jackson offered several aims for Operation PUSH: form an economic plan for black and poor people, devise alternatives to welfare and prison, revive the labor movement, create a bill of rights for veterans, and provide adequate health care for all Americans. All thirty-five Operation Breadbasket staff members, and twenty

Jesse Jackson announces an agreement between Operation PUSH and Avon Products, Inc. for the creation of a $59 million program to foster increased opportunities for minority groups.

of the twenty-five board members, left Breadbasket to join PUSH.

Operation PUSH was not an immediate success, partly because the organization did not always run smoothly. Though Jackson was a man of broad vision, he was not good with details. He expected others to know what he wanted and get it done. At the same time, he placed high demands on his staff. The stress caused many staff members to quit.

Slowly, however, Operation PUSH achieved successes. Using his powers of persuasion, Jackson convinced one company after another to hire, train, and promote minorities. The Ford Motor Company increased its minority dealerships from 30 to over 250. General Foods hired 360 blacks and other minorities for jobs at all levels, increased deposits in black-owned banks by five hundred thousand, and began using black-owned advertising agencies, law firms, and construction companies. Other companies, including Burger King, 7-Eleven, Avon, and Quaker Oats, also agreed to change the way they did business.

Operation PUSH did not confine its efforts to business. The organization also fought welfare cuts in state capitals and pressed for higher teaching standards. As the organization grew, Jackson was making over one hundred speeches and television appearances a year.

Entry into Politics

As successful as Operation PUSH was, few average Americans knew much about it. Only business leaders knew what Jackson was doing. Jackson felt confined. Working "inside" was not his style. He felt his talents were not being used to their fullest. To make a bigger impact, Jackson needed a bigger stage. Politics provided that platform.

Jesse Jackson speaks at a voter registration drive in Yonkers, New York.

In the early 1970s Jackson began to help register voters. He also campaigned for black politicians. He gave his support to several black mayoral candidates, including Carl Stokes in Cleveland; Kenneth Gibson in Newark, New Jersey; and Richard Hatcher in Gary, Indiana. All won and gratefully acknowledged Jackson's support.

The more famous Jackson became, the more people asked him to speak. Jackson roamed the country, traveling more than two hundred thousand miles a year. He led marches for economic justice, organized seminars on tax reform, and conferred with President Gerald Ford about the needs of minorities. In Chicago he worked for the selection of a black superintendent of schools and chief of police.

A Message to Black Youths

Because of the difficulties he faced growing up, Jackson has always had a special rapport with young people. To youthful audiences, Jackson pushed a message for self-respect and against vandalism, drugs, teenage pregnancies, and dropouts. He told black youths that they were getting the wrong message from people they looked up to—and that they themselves were partly to blame. He said, "Kids walk around not with books under their arms but with radios up against their heads. Children can't read and write, but they can memorize whole albums." [71]

He also told high school boys,

> Brothers, you're not a man because you can kill somebody. You're not a man because you can make a baby. They can make babies through artificial insemination. Imbeciles can make babies. Fools can make babies. You're a man only if you can raise a baby, protect a baby and provide for a baby. [72]

To girls, he added,

> There's another side to it, sisters. If you are to deserve the kind of man you cheer for, you cannot spend more time in school on the cultivation of your bosom than your books. If you are to be the right kind of woman,

you cannot have a fully developed bottom and a half developed brain. A donkey got an ass, but he ain't got no
sense.[73]

Standing outside a school named for Martin Luther King Jr.,
Jackson saw a group of students shooting craps. He felt dis-
gusted, but it sparked the idea for PUSH for Excellence, soon
shortened to PUSH-Excel. This was a national project challenging minority youths to take advantage of the current changes in
race relations. Jackson asked,

> What does it matter if the doors of opportunity are now
> wide open if you still too uneducated to find your way
> through that door? If you too high or drunk to stagger
> through it? What does it matter if we won the right to
> equal schooling if you've lost the will to learn?[74]

A 1976 *60 Minutes* profile of PUSH-Excel brought it national
attention. Within two years the program earned government
and foundation grants worth $2 million. It expanded to thirty-
five schools in nine cities.

The PUSH-Excel program succeeded in lowering absen-
teeism, improving morale, and increasing student performance.
A Los Angeles teacher said, "The program has turned kids
around. I see a difference in their attitudes, the way they dress,
and the way they relate to me. Jackson has made the teachers an
extension of himself, and when a student sees me, he or she is
looking at Jackson."[75]

Jackson's ability to connect with audiences about the issues
of the day earned him the respect and admiration of President
Jimmy Carter. In 1979 the president invited Jackson to Camp
David to confer about problems of the American spirit. The
next year Jackson campaigned in seventy-two cities for the
Democratic ticket. Jackson also traveled to Africa and the
Middle East to discuss issues of peace, human rights, and eco-
nomic development. A 1983 American Broadcasting Company
(ABC) poll found that more African Americans identified
Jackson as their leader than anyone else. He led second-place
Andrew Young by forty-three points.

A Challenge to Youth

Jesse Jackson never hesitates to challenge all his listeners, including teenagers. In this quote from Marshall Frady's *Jesse: The Life and Pilgrimage of Jesse Jackson*, he urges teenagers at a PUSH-Excel rally to take charge of their lives.

> There is a challenge *beyond* opportunity. The victim is not responsible for being down, but the victim *is* responsible for getting back up. If you can't read or write or do math, well, people will pity you, but they won't hire you. We have to *fight* our way up out of poverty, and excellence is our weapon. We must, by the will of our dignity, be more sober, more serious, more determined than our oppressors. It's the only way we will ever break out.

During the 1970s, Jesse Jackson often opened his speeches to students, and his Saturday morning addresses at Operation PUSH's community forum, with a chant. It is excerpted from Jackson's book *Straight from the Heart.*

> I am somebody.
>
> I may be poor, but I am somebody.
>
> I may be uneducated, I may be unskilled, but I am somebody.
>
> I may be on welfare, I may be prematurely pregnant, I may be on drugs, I may be victimized by racism, but I am somebody.
>
> Respect me. Protect me. Never neglect me. I am God's child.

Jesse Jackson was clearly the most important black political figure in the United States, but he aspired to more. He wanted to lead not just the black community but also the entire nation. As 1984 approached, he would try to do just that.

Chapter 5

The First Presidential Campaign

ALL HIS LIFE, Jesse Jackson lived by his grandmother's adage "Ain't no such word as *cain't*." [76] He never accepted the notion that there were limits to what he could do. This was especially true of limits based on the color of his skin. He knew that racial discrimination existed; he simply refused to accept it as a force in his life, to give it power over him. Calvin Morris, one of Jackson's college friends, remembered this as Jackson's most singular quality:

> He thought globally about himself, saw himself in places that young Negro boys like ourselves had never considered. I mean, I saw myself maybe as a college president, that was the biggest thing. Jesse saw himself as a president of the United States! Which was crazy! But that's the kind of sense of his own destiny that he had. [77]

As early as sixth grade, Jesse Jackson had dreamed of becoming the president of the United States. As his fame grew, he began to think seriously about running for the highest office in the land. Others might say it was impossible for a black man to be elected president, but Jackson had never listened to the voices that said "cain't," and he never would.

Jackson had campaigned hard for the Democratic ticket in 1980, and his efforts undoubtedly helped President Jimmy Carter close the gap between himself and Ronald Reagan, who had led in the polls for months before the election. Nevertheless, Reagan, a man whose policies Jackson deplored, won.

Ronald Reagan defeated Jimmy Carter in the 1980 presidential election and became the fortieth president of the United States.

After the election, Jackson continued to speak out against President Reagan and his policies. As Jackson toured the country on behalf of PUSH-Excel, he kept in contact with the political contacts he had made during the Carter campaign. As the 1984 election approached, Jackson began to devote more of his time to helping the Democratic Party recapture the White House. In the summer of 1983, Jackson toured six southern states, appearing at up to forty rallies a week. He talked about the rise in black poverty and unemployment during the first three years of the Reagan administration. He urged African Americans to register to vote so they could participate in the upcoming presidential election. "There's a freedom train a-coming!" he shouted. "But you got to be registered to ride. Get on board! Get on board!"[78]

Jackson was not the only one with a message; his audiences had a message for him as well. Throughout the tour, audiences

Jesse Jackson gives a "thumbs up" salute to delegates of the First National Assembly of Black Church Organizations in New Orleans in 1984.

chanted "Run, Jesse, run!" Famous Americans and common citizens alike urged the gifted speaker from Greenville, South Carolina, to run for president. His early supporters included black mayors like Marion Barry of Washington, D.C., Ernest Morial of New Orleans, and Richard Hatcher of Gary, Indiana; members of the Congressional Black Caucus; and Shirley Chisholm, a retired New York congresswoman who in 1972 became the first African American to make a serious run for the presidency. Former U.S. attorney general Ramsey Clark, a white man, also backed Jackson.

Other voices counseled Jackson not to run. Many black leaders opposed Jackson's entry into the race, either because they thought another nominee had a better chance of beating President Reagan or because they simply did not like Jackson. California Assembly speaker Willie Brown, mayors Coleman Young of Detroit and Tom Bradley of Los Angeles, and even Jackson's old ally Andrew Young of Atlanta opposed the Jackson candidacy and spoke against it. They supported Walter Mondale, the former vice president to President Carter, as a more "electable" candidate than Jackson. They worried that Jackson's candidacy would divide the party and make it harder for any Democrat to be elected in the fall.

An Underdog Race

Jackson ignored those who said he could not win. On November 3, 1983, he entered the race. Even though the general election was still a year away, Jackson was the last Democrat to declare his candidacy. By the time he announced that he was running, other candidates had raised more money, better organized their staffs, and opened campaign offices in important states. Jackson had a lot of catching up to do.

Jackson found that many of the Democratic Party's primary rules worked against a candidate with a small following. In most states, a candidate needed 20 percent of the vote in a congressional district to qualify for even one delegate. The rule was designed to prevent candidates with few supporters from diverting the energy and resources at the convention, but it also placed a burden on a campaign like Jackson's, which was starting out small. Other states had winner-take-all rules, in which the top vote-getter in a congressional district or an entire state got all of the delegates.

As a result of the primary rules, Jackson decided to concentrate on states with large black populations and on cities with high numbers of black voters. Most of the states that Jackson targeted, such as his home state of South Carolina, were in the South. Most of the cities, such as Chicago, were in the North.

Although Jackson's campaign was designed to create a base of support among blacks, Jackson saw himself as a candidate for all voters who felt left out of government—people he called "the desperate, the damned, the disinherited, the disrespected and the despised."[79] He planned to fight for policies and programs that would help not only blacks but also Hispanics, Native Americans, feminists, college students, environmentalists, peace activists, and farmers. Borrowing a phrase from the Poor People's Campaign, he called his constituency the Rainbow Coalition.

Reporters covering the Jackson campaign seemed to concentrate on Jackson's race. At one point Jackson complained,

> The news media says every night, "Jesse Jackson, black leader." It never says "Walter Mondale, white leader." "Gary Hart, white leader." The reinforcement of the blackness almost makes whites feel excluded, unwelcome, and that's a double standard. I mean, why should the media keep referring to me as a black leader? My blackness is self-evident.[80]

Comments like these may have hurt Jackson more than they helped him. Many reporters believed that the title "black leader" was appropriate for Jackson since he was only the second black person to seek the presidency and since he was not an elected official with a title such as "senator," "governor," or even "mayor." It seemed to some that it was Jackson, not the media, who was making race an issue. Up to that point in his career, Jackson had benefited from a generally positive treatment in the press. By attacking the media's portrayal of him, however, Jackson alienated some members of the press.

The issue of race actually benefited Jackson in some ways. His opponents faced a dilemma: If they attacked his positions on issues, they risked being called racist. If they did not attack, they opened themselves up to the charge of giving him preferential treatment based on race. Few political insiders thought that Jackson had a chance of being nominated, but everyone knew that he was bringing millions of people into the Democratic Party. No candidate could afford to alienate Jackson or his followers.

Compared to the campaigns of the other candidates, Jackson's campaign was disorganized and low budget. His opponents could afford to hire veteran campaign workers, but Jackson had to make do with volunteers who had never run a presidential campaign. His foes flew on chartered jets and stayed in the best hotels. Jackson flew in old prop planes and stayed in the homes of his supporters.

Jackson's campaign may have lacked many things, but it had one important asset the others did not: Jackson himself. His message was clear, he offered new perspectives on old issues, and his speaking skills were engaging.

Jackson possessed another quality that the other candidates lacked: daring. While the other candidates took polls to test what the voters would think of their every move, Jackson took action. For example, two months before the first primary election, Jackson traveled to the Middle East to see if he could secure the release of an American pilot who had been shot down over Syria. The pilot, Lieutenant Robert O. Goodman Jr., had been flying on a mission to support ground troops that President Reagan had sent into the neighboring country of Lebanon. The Syrians said they would

A day after announcing his candidacy for president in 1984, Jesse Jackson exhorts his supporters in Washington, D.C., to help him secure the Democratic nomination.

A Man Like No Other

Political reporters did not always know what to make of Jesse Jackson. Bob Faw and Nancy Skelton, who traveled with him in 1984, describe their reactions in *Thunder in America*.

> He was always accessible, often too much so. The more we saw and listened, the more we came to respect—and to distrust him. His words could hypnotize, but we learned that very little he said could be taken at face value. One minute he could be childish; the next, profound. He could infuriate and inspire, could savage egos or make the downtrodden feel more important than ever before; he was as exasperating as he was endearing. Sometimes we applauded, and other times we cursed.
>
> Still, his instinct for survival, his showmanship, his quick wit and lightning reflexes were like no other public figures we'd ever met. Even when repulsed, we were always fascinated. Whatever we might think, we could always marvel at him. Finally we realized that our reactions were ambivalent, even contradictory, because there is no *one* Jesse Jackson. That his quicksilver personality constantly adapts, forges ahead; that he operates on different levels at different times. And that each is an authentic Jesse Jackson.

hold the twenty-seven-year-old black navy pilot until the United States withdrew troops from Lebanon. On Christmas Day 1983 Jackson left for Damascus, the capital of Syria. On his plane were staff members, journalists, his two oldest sons, Secret Service agents, and several religious figures. One of the people who accompanied Jackson was Louis Farrakhan, the high minister of the Nation of Islam. Jackson hoped that the presence of Farrakhan, one of America's leading Muslims, would help convince the Syrians, who also were Muslims, to negotiate.

The Syrians permitted Jackson to visit Goodman in his cell. Jackson gave Goodman a Bible and a letter from Goodman's mother. In a meeting with Syrian president Hafez al-Assad, Jackson appealed for Goodman's release. To the surprise of many, al-Assad, a leader generally hostile toward the United States, agreed to free the pilot. Jackson returned to Washington with Goodman at his side.

Since Jackson was not an official representative of the United States, many Americans questioned the wisdom of his mission. Some worried that he said things in his meeting with al-Assad that might conflict with government policy. Others wondered about his motives for going to Syria. They questioned whether his main interest was freeing Goodman or drawing attention to himself. The *New York Times* called Jackson "a skillful self-promoter."[81] President Reagan said only, "You don't quarrel with success."[82]

Jesse Jackson poses with Lt. Robert O. Goodman, a U.S. Navy pilot who was shot down over Syria. In the midst of his 1984 presidential campaign, Jackson flew to Syria to negotiate Goodman's release.

Another Kind of Racism

Jackson's freewheeling style won him many supporters, but it also proved to be a liability. Three weeks after Goodman's release, while chatting with two black reporters in an airport cafeteria, Jackson referred to New York City as "Hymie-town," an unflattering reference to the city's large Jewish population. Nineteen days later one of those reporters included the remark in a report about Jackson. The press pounced on the story. Overnight, everyone in the country who followed the news knew what Jackson had said. "It was like somebody dropped an atomic bomb right in the middle of our campaign,"[83] said Richard Hatcher.

At first Jackson denied making the comments. Then he said he could not remember whether he made them. Suddenly, the man who had crusaded against racism had to answer for his own racial comment. Two days before the New Hampshire presidential primary, Jackson apologized at a synagogue in Manchester.

Despite the apology, the attacks continued. People recalled that several years earlier, on a trip to the Mideast, Jackson had embraced Palestine Liberation Organization leader Yasir Arafat, a sworn enemy of the state of Israel. They also remembered that Louis Farrakhan, who once called Judaism a "gutter religion,"[84] had traveled with Jackson on the trip to free Robert Goodman.

Jackson fought back. He reminded the public that he had worked with many different groups throughout his career and that he had even marched against neo-Nazis in Skokie, Illinois. Even Jackson's considerable powers of persuasion could not undo the damage. His popularity plummeted. He had been predicted to get as much as 16 percent of the vote in the nation's first primary in New Hampshire—a state whose population was only 1 percent black—but instead he finished with a little over 5 percent.

Gaining Delegates

When the presidential primaries and caucuses shifted to the South, Jackson did better. He won the primary in his home state of South Carolina. He also won in Virginia. He finished second in five other states. In Arkansas, where he spent only a day and a half campaigning and had no money or official organization, he finished a strong second. He got 34 percent of the vote, just two percentage points behind front-runner Walter Mondale. However, because of the primary rules, he won only six Arkansas delegates. Walter Mondale earned twenty, while third-place finisher Gary Hart got nine.

Jackson's southern strategy worked well, but his northern strategy did not. His remark about New York City Jews cost him

Jesse Jackson embraces Yasir Arafat in 1983. Jackson's relationship with Arafat, an avowed enemy of Israel at the time, made it difficult for Jackson to refute charges of being anti-Semitic.

support in that city as well as in other northern cities. When the voting was over, Jackson had finished third behind Walter Mondale and Gary Hart.

Still, Jackson's campaign had surpassed nearly everyone's expectations. Overall he won 21 percent of all primary and caucus votes, including 80 percent of black voters. He carried forty-one congressional districts and seven major cities. Of the eight Democratic candidates who started the race, he finished third. He spent less than $3 million, while Mondale spent $31 million and Hart $17 million. New York governor Mario Cuomo said admiringly, "When they write the history of this (primary campaign), the longest chapter will be on Jackson. The man didn't have two cents. He didn't have one television or radio ad. And look what he did."[85]

The San Francisco Convention

When the 1984 Democratic National Convention began in San Francisco, Mondale was virtually assured of the nomination. Yet drama hung in the air; everyone knew that Jackson wanted to play a role in the convention, but no one was sure what that role would be. Some people thought he wanted to be nominated for vice president. Others thought he wanted the party to change its rules for primary elections or delegate selection. Some people predicted that Jackson would stage a walk-out or mass protest over the primary rules. Jackson quashed these rumors, saying he would not walk out because "I've always fought to get *in*."[86]

After a series of high-level negotiations, Democratic Party officials agreed to let Jackson speak the night before Walter Mondale would be nominated for president. Most of Jackson's fifty-minute speech was dedicated to the themes he had repeated throughout the 1984 presidential race. This time, however, he had a national audience. Millions of Americans listened, spellbound.

When Jackson spoke, he described what he had learned during the campaign. "Leaders must be tough enough to fight, tender enough to cry, human enough to make mistakes, humble enough to admit them, strong enough to absorb the pain and resilient enough to bounce back and keep on moving,"[87] he said.

"Shared Blood and Shared Sacrifices"

In his famous speech at the 1984 Democratic National Convention, which was included in Jackson's book *Straight from the Heart,* Jesse Jackson reached out to members of every religion.

We are co-partners in a long and rich religious history—the Judeo-Christian traditions. Many blacks and Jews have a shared passion for social justice at home and peace abroad. We must seek a revival of the spirit, inspired by a new vision and new possibilities. We must return to higher ground.

We are bound by Moses and Jesus, but also connected with Islam and Mohammed. These three great religions, Judaism, Christianity and Islam, were all born in the revered and holy city of Jerusalem.

We are bound by Dr. Martin Luther King Jr. and [by American theologian] Rabbi Abraham Heschel. . . . We are bound by shared blood and shared sacrifices. . . . We must turn from finger-pointing to clasped hands. We must share our burdens and our joys with each other once again. We must turn to each other and not on each other, and choose higher ground.

He once again expressed regret for his remarks about New York City: "If, in my low moments, in word, deed or attitude, through some error of temper, taste or tone, I have caused anyone discomfort, created pain or revived someone's fears, that was not my truest self." [88]

He described his vision of America as a nation of small, diverse parts that is united with common purpose:

Our flag is red, white and blue, but our nation is a rainbow—red, yellow, brown, black and white—and we're all precious in God's sight. America is not like a blanket—one piece of unbroken cloth, the same color, the same texture, the same size. America is more like a quilt—many patches, many pieces, many colors, many sizes, all woven and held together by a common thread. . . . Even in our fractured state, all of us count and all of us fit somewhere. We have proven that we can survive without each other. But we have not proven that we can win and progress without each other. We must come together. [89]

Andrew Young, his former ally who more recently opposed Jackson's run for president, called it "probably the best speech he'd ever done. It was very carefully crafted. It said what needed to be said. And I wrote him that Martin [Luther King Jr.] would be very proud of him."[90]

A Tireless Campaigner

The next day the Democrats nominated Walter Mondale for president and Geraldine Ferraro for vice president. Just as he had four years before, Jackson campaigned hard for the Democratic ticket, traveling more miles than either Mondale or Ferraro. His own campaign had only sharpened his skills as an orator. John White, the former Democratic Party national chairman, heard Jackson speak in Texas, and marveled:

> Within less than 10 minutes he had those old West Texas and East Texas boys and these were *not* Jesse's people— had them standing on their chairs, waving their straw hats and cheering. I'd seen some of the best political speakers in this country . . . but I've never seen anybody take a basically hostile crowd like that and get the cheers that he got. . . . It was phenomenal.[91]

Despite Jackson's efforts, Ronald Reagan easily defeated Mondale. Although the Democrats had once again lost the White House, they still had much to celebrate. A record number of blacks—10 million in all—helped the party win many local contests. More black mayors were elected than in any year since 1970. As a man who had spent many years working on a local level, Jackson understood better than most the impact that his own campaign had on the country. "If you can get your share of legislators, mayors, sheriffs, school-board members, tax assessors and dog catchers, you can live with whoever is in the White House,"[92] he observed.

Jackson's campaign for president failed to put him in the White House, but it opened many other doors. Business leaders, Hollywood celebrities, and world leaders sought meetings with him. He had an audience with Pope John Paul II. He talked to

Pope John Paul II welcomes Jesse Jackson to the Vatican on June 23, 1999. Jackson emerged from his first presidential campaign as a widely respected humanitarian.

Soviet leader Mikhail Gorbachev about the plight of Soviet Jews. Through the Rainbow Coalition, he fought for education and social justice in the United States. He led demonstrations by workers protesting the closing of a steel plant. He helped farmers who were losing their land. He even found time to host the popular television program *Saturday Night Live.*

He also started planning his second run for President of the United States.

Chapter 6

A Second Try

THE FIRST TIME Jesse Jackson ran for president, many people wondered why he was doing it. They assumed he was trying to promote a cause, prove a point, or shake up the system. Few guessed that he actually was running to win. Four years later, when Jackson again sought the presidency, everyone knew he wanted to win. The question was, could he really do it?

After his 1984 presidential campaign, Jackson's star shone brighter than ever. A poll of Americans showed him to be more esteemed than anyone except President Ronald Reagan and Pope John Paul II. Another poll, taken in the spring of 1987, asked Democratic voters for their preference for president in the 1988 election. Jackson placed first, six points ahead of Massachusetts governor Michael Dukakis.

Not everyone agreed with Jackson's politics or favored his personal style, of course. But some opposed him for one basic reason: the color of his skin. One poll showed that 23 percent of all white voters would not consider voting for any black candidate.

A Different Campaign

The polls meant little to Jackson. He had already decided to run for office, and he planned to run his second campaign differently from his first. In addition to getting an earlier start, Jackson emphasized different issues. His speeches focused on economic issues more than racial ones. He pursued white votes even more eagerly than he did in 1984. He distanced himself from Louis Farrakhan, the controversial Nation of Islam leader. Instead, he enlisted the support of Bill Cosby, a man journalist Howard

Fineman referred to as "one of the most popular men in America and a symbol of black middle-class aspirations."[93]

Wherever Jackson campaigned, he talked about the problems facing Americans of all races. He pointed out that American companies were firing workers in order to hire

Wearing a cap from the United Auto Workers union, Jesse Jackson campaigns for president outside a General Motors automobile plant in Tarrytown, New York, in April 1988.

cheaper labor abroad, millions of citizens lacked health insurance, public schools were deteriorating, the environment was in trouble, farmers were losing their land, and gays and lesbians lacked legal protection.

Jackson's message made sense to many people, even those who had once doubted Jackson's sincerity. *Ebony* magazine described a meeting in Memphis that was filled with "tattoo-wearing, beer-drinking, truck-driving Southern good ol' boys. [These men who] just five years ago would have cursed his name now push their way to the front just to shake his hand."[94] At many of his campaign stops, the call of 1984—"Run, Jesse, run!"—turned into "Win, Jesse, win!"

The first real test of Jackson's new campaign came in Iowa, where voters express their preferences in party meetings known as caucuses. Jackson had set up his Iowa headquarters in the small town of Greenfield rather than the big city of Des Moines. He wanted to prove to the state that he understood the problems of farmers and other "little people." His concern impressed Iowa voters. Though only 1 percent of Iowa's population is black, Jackson received 10 percent of the vote. Jackson did not come close to winning, but he proved that he could attract a large number of white voters to his campaign.

The same thing happened in New Hampshire, another state with a small black population. Jackson again won 10 percent of the vote. In Minnesota—a state that was 2 percent black—Jackson finished second, this time with 20 percent of the vote. His momentum surged. Jackson placed second in Maine, earning 30 percent of the vote, and first in Vermont.

Super Tuesday

March 8, 1988, brought "Super Tuesday," when several southern states hold primary elections together. Party leaders had originally planned the calendar that way so that voters in the traditionally conservative South could slow any liberal candidate who had done well in the early stage of the campaign. As in the 1984 campaign, Jackson campaigned hard in the southern states that formed his political base. This time, Jackson finished first in five states and second in nine others, winning 27 percent of the vote. He took nearly one-third of all southern delegates.

When "Super Tuesday" was over, Jackson found himself in the middle of a three-way race. His only remaining opponents were Massachusetts governor Michael Dukakis and Tennessee senator Albert Gore. Suddenly, the 1988 race was unlike any presidential campaign before. An African American man was creating excitement all across the country. "Mention the name of any other candidate and you don't generate enough electricity to light a refrigerator bulb," said Democratic pollster Peter Hart. "Mention Jesse Jackson and the energy fills the room."[95]

Tennessee senator Al Gore (above) and Massachusetts governor Michael Dukakis (left) vied with Jesse Jackson for the Democratic presidential nomination in 1988.

A seventy-three-year-old white woman spoke for many when she said she was amazed to find herself voting for a black man. However, she noted, "He's down to earth, an honest man. We need a break for the working people." [96]

Buoyed by Super Tuesday, the Jackson campaign stormed into Michigan. Traditionally a conservative state, Michigan is also home to a large black population concentrated in Detroit. Blacks turned out in record numbers to support Jackson, but he also drew 20 percent of the white vote, four times better than he had done in 1984. He won the primary with an astonishing 55 percent of the vote. Governor Dukakis lagged twenty-seven percentage points behind. *Time* magazine put him on the cover with just a single word that expressed both excitement and questions: "Jesse!?" [97]

The next week Jackson drew large crowds in Wisconsin, a predominantly white state. The *New York Times* reported, "Let it be recorded that for at least one week in American history, in a middle-sized Midwestern state, a broad range of white voters took the Presidential candidacy of a black man with utmost seriousness." [98]

Throughout Wisconsin, voters of all races turned out in large numbers at Jackson's rallies. White union women wore Jackson T-shirts. In a barn in rural Janesville, "Parents held up children to see, blond teenage girls giggled over his good looks, skeptics were drawn in, and by the end of the address, the crowd was chanting, 'Win, Jesse, win!'" [99]

The question mark on the *Time* magazine cover hinted at a question that hung over Jackson's surging candidacy: Was the nation really willing to elect a black candidate as president? Rather than discuss this question openly, many people sought to discredit Jackson based on things other than his race. As Bert Lance, a former Carter administration official from Georgia who became one of Jackson's first white campaign advisers, observed,

> None of us wants to be a racist, so we look to see if some other circumstance can allow us to say to ourselves, "Well, I'm not doing this because he is black, but because of these other circumstances"—and we cleanse ourselves and we're free to go ahead (and vote for someone else). And God knows, Jesse gave them a lot of opportunities to do that. [100]

Whether it was his controversial remarks about Jews four years earlier, his embrace of Yasir Arafat, his conduct after Martin Luther King Jr.'s assassination, or the allegations about his poor management of Operation PUSH, Jackson's past gave voters ample reason to oppose him. At the same time, Jackson's campaign efforts were not as well organized in Wisconsin as they had been in other states. When the votes were counted, Governor Dukakis beat Jackson 48 percent to 28 percent.

New York: Turning Point

The setback in Wisconsin was disappointing, but Jackson put it behind him and focused on the New York primary. In New York, Jackson had to battle his own past as much as his current opponents. Outspoken New York City mayor Edward I. Koch, a Jew, had publicly opposed Jackson ever since publication of Jackson's derogatory description of New York City's Jewish population. Mayor Koch called himself "Paul Revere," and said he had to "alert New York and the nation to Jackson's true menace."[101] He

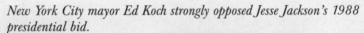

New York City mayor Ed Koch strongly opposed Jesse Jackson's 1988 presidential bid.

said that Jews—who made up a significant number of New York City voters—would be crazy to vote for Jackson. A few prominent Jews, including author Norman Mailer and Democratic Party official Ann Lewis, rushed to Jackson's defense, pointing out his support for Russian Jews and his frequent calls for dialogue between blacks and Jews. But Mayor Koch's words had a great impact on many voters. When Jackson declined to address Jewish groups or walk in the Salute to Israel Day parade, he lost even more votes.

Despite Mayor Koch's efforts, Jackson carried New York City, winning 98 percent of the black vote and 63 percent of the Hispanic vote. When the votes for the entire state were counted, however, Governor Dukakis came out on top, winning 51 percent of the vote to Jackson's 37 percent. Senator Gore received only 10 percent and dropped out of the race.

Jackson's speech that night was gracious. He was ready for a two-man battle with Governor Dukakis, but the race never got started. Fearing that a black nominee would fail to draw large numbers of white voters to the polls, Democratic politicians across the country voiced their support for Dukakis. As the endorsements piled up, Dukakis won primaries in Pennsylvania,

The Speechwriter at Work

Bob Borosage, a key adviser in the 1988 presidential campaign, was asked on the PBS television show *Frontline*, "The Pilgrimage of Jesse Jackson," to describe the genius of Jackson's speechwriting.

The lines that Jackson uses are Jackson lines. He would spend time in the airplane [and] between speeches often listening to jazz on a set of earphones. He'd play the jazz recording and while he was doing that, he would be what he calls Jacksonizing—all this information that he'd be taking in and all the impressions that he'd have.

And then about once every other day, you'd see him pull out a yellow pad and he would write in almost illegible scribbles, a line of argument down the side of the page. And it would be . . . talking points and metaphors that he had distilled in the course of this thinking. And when you saw him do that, you knew he was about to produce a new riff, a new set of images. A new one-liner that was going to crystallize something that was on his mind.

New Jersey, and California, assuring himself the Democratic nomination.

When the primary season was over, Jackson had finished second. His 7 million votes were the most for any second-place finisher in history. Two million of those votes were cast by white voters. He headed to the Democratic National Convention in Atlanta with over twelve hundred delegates, nearly one-third of the total.

The Atlanta Convention

Second-place finishers in the primaries are often offered the second spot on the presidential ticket. For example, John Kennedy picked second-place finisher Lyndon Johnson for his running mate, and Ronald Reagan picked second-place finisher George Bush. Offering the vice presidency to the runner-up not only seems democratic and fair, but it also brings unity to the party. For these reasons, Jackson thought that Dukakis should and would name him as the vice presidential candidate. He felt he had earned the position.

Most political observers believed that would never happen. No presidential candidate ever wants to be overshadowed by his vice president, they reasoned, and Jackson's physical presence and personal style simply overpowered Michael Dukakis. In the days before the 1988 Democratic National Convention in Atlanta, Dukakis did nothing to dispel Jackson's hopes nor to confirm them.

Jackson's arrival in Atlanta was as unconventional as his campaign. He rode from Chicago in a "Rainbow Express" caravan of seven buses, picking up delegates (and television coverage) along the seven-day, nine-city route. Jackson knew he was on the list of seven semifinalists for vice president. He asked Dukakis to tell him privately when the decision was made. That call never came. Instead, Jackson learned he would not be selected in a roundabout, public way. Jackson was offended and embarrassed that Dukakis had not told him personally. Jackson used slave references to explain his anger and hurt: "I cannot be asked to go out into the field, pick up voters, bale them up, and deliver them to the big house where policy is made and not be a part of the equation. We want partnership, equity and shared responsibility." [102]

Even so, Jackson did not want to be seen as a dividing force in the Democratic Party. Two days before the convention began, he addressed thousands of supporters in a park. He urged them to be calm. "We don't have to march to protest outside the convention hall, we have seats inside now. . . . We're here now to build from the inside out, rather than sack the place from the outside in." [103]

Another Historic Speech

Leaders of the Democratic Party asked Jackson to address the entire delegation and a national television audience. The speech was not only the most memorable of the convention, it was also the most memorable of recent political history.

Jackson saluted Dukakis. "His foreparents came to America on immigrant ships. My foreparents came to America on slave ships. But whatever the original ships, we are both in the same boat now." [104] He also honored the memory of Martin Luther King Jr., buried just a few miles from the convention center, and the many men and women—black, white, brown, and yellow—who fought and died in the struggle for freedom and social justice.

He gave a powerful, emotional account of his childhood in South Carolina. He said, "I was born in the slum, but the slum was not born in me. And it wasn't born in you, and you can make it." [105]

Speaking directly to the poor and powerless people watching on television sets around the world (the speech was carried live in Africa, where it was 4:00 A.M.), Jackson explained why he remained in the race to the end.

> When my name goes in nomination, your name goes in nomination. Wherever you are tonight, you can make it. Hold your head high. Stick your chest out. You can make it. It gets dark sometimes, but the morning comes. . . . Keep hope alive! [106]

Jesse Jackson and Michael Dukakis greet a crowd during the 1988 presidential campaign. Though disappointed that Dukakis did not select him as his running mate, Jackson campaigned for the Democratic nominee.

Jackson's speech was interrupted for applause fifty-five times. There were eighteen standing ovations. When it was over, friends and enemies alike praised Jackson for the inspiring message of hope he delivered with such eloquence and passion.

The General Election

For the third presidential campaign in a row, Jackson worked tirelessly for the Democratic ticket. Once again, Jackson claimed to have traveled more miles than either the presidential or vice presidential candidate. He helped register new voters. The result

Never Stop Dreaming

Jackson's memorable speech at the 1988 Democratic National Convention is included in *Straight from the Heart.*

> Most poor people are not lazy. They are not black. They are not brown. They are mostly white and female and young. But whether white, black or brown, a hungry baby's belly turned inside out is the same color—color it pain, color it hurt, color it agony.
>
> Most poor people are not on welfare. Some of them are illiterate and can't read the want-ad sections. And when they can, they can't find a job that matches the address. They work hard every day. I know, I live amongst them. They catch the early bus. They work every day. They raise other people's children. They work every day.
>
> They clean the streets. They work every day. They drive dangerous cabs. They change the beds you slept in those hotels last night, and can't get a union contract. They work every day. . . .
>
> You must never stop dreaming. . . . Dream of teachers who teach for life and not for a living. Dream of doctors who are concerned more about public health than private wealth. Dream of lawyers more concerned about justice than a judgeship. Dream of preachers who are concerned more about prophecy than profiteering. Dream on the high road with sound values.

was the same, however. In November 1988 George Bush was elected president in the largest electoral landslide in history. The professional politicians who had feared that a Jackson candidacy might drag down the entire party found that Dukakis carried just two states. They had helped create their own debacle.

Most experts believe that the 1988 election simply confirmed what the previous two elections had shown: Even though most voters were registered Democrats, they did not support traditional Democratic policies. Some observers saw something new in the 1988 election, however. Hendrik Hertzberg wrote that the 1988 election was one of the most important of American history, and the reason was not Michael Dukakis or George Bush—it was Jesse Jackson.

Fifty years from now his name and deeds will be known to every educated or half-educated American. . . . Among (black leaders) he is exceeded in fame and impact only by Martin Luther King Jr. and possibly Booker T. Washington. It is as certain as such things can be that he will be seen as a larger historical figure than such past leaders of the black masses as Frederick Douglass, Marcus Garvey, or Malcolm X.[107]

In his quest for the presidency, Jesse Jackson finally achieved the status, recognition, and fame he had always sought. He had

Jesse Jackson acknowledges his supporters as he campaigns in Los Angeles, California. Jackson's fame and prestige were enhanced by his strong showing in the 1988 presidential campaign.

A Complex Man

Many political writers tried to analyze the various sides of Jesse Jackson. Shortly before the Democratic National Convention, political writer Stanley Crouch wrote about Jackson in the *New Republic*.

> Jesse Jackson can do things no other politician of comparable stature can. He has ventured into areas of criticism only he can inhabit. . . . He has challenged Negroes to get off dope, to raise the babies they make, to stop being lackadaisical in school—to work their way out of problems rather than whine as they sullenly accept them. Any white politician so bold would be shouted down as a racist, or told that he or she didn't understand the dictates of Afro-American culture. . . .

> But for all the light that the radiant reverend offers at this time in our history, there is an undeniable element of darkness, ice-cold questions about his character and his methods, proof that he is a breathing idol who has, if not feet of clay, a good amount of thick mud on his shoes. Jesse Jackson is a man besmirched by his own conduct—by his raw ambition and his willingness to make pretzels out of the truth. So many welcome and unwelcome things in one man are hard to reconcile.

not gained the power of the presidency, but he had acquired a different power, a moral power. He was not in position to change the law, but he could fulfill the mission he had discussed with professor Samuel Proctor twenty-five years earlier—to change society in deeper ways than even the law would allow. Jackson's crusade to make the country better had not ended with the 1988 election. It had begun.

Chapter 7

"A Citizen of the World"

Most unsuccessful candidates for the presidency quietly drift out of the public eye. This has certainly been the case of Jesse Jackson's chief rivals for the Democratic nomination. Walter Mondale, Gary Hart, and Michael Dukakis have virtually disappeared from public life. Jackson, however, has not. He continues to make headlines and, more importantly, to make history.

In 1989 Jackson moved to Washington, D.C., not to occupy the White House, but because so much of his work was now taking place in the nation's capital. His move fueled speculation that he planned to run for mayor of Washington. Jackson knew that his temperament was not suited to the administrative details all mayors must attend to, and he decided not to run. For a while his name was mentioned as a possibility for the chairmanship of the National Association for the Advancement of Colored People (NAACP), but Jackson had moved beyond the arena of civil rights. As the 1990s began, he was seen as a leader for social justice, a voice for oppressed people around the globe.

Suddenly Jackson seemed to be everywhere at once. Each week he hosted a discussion program on television. He led rallies in support of such causes as improving police conduct and providing greater housing opportunities for minorities. And he continued to travel.

Another Hostage Release

In August 1990, during the early weeks of the Persian Gulf crisis, Jackson journeyed to Iraq. His goal was to secure the release of foreign citizens being held hostage by the Iraqis. To the surprise of many, Jackson persuaded Iraqi leader Saddam Hussein to free hundreds of women and children, as well as five men, imprisoned in Baghdad. Saddam then went even further, releasing hostages in Kuwait. The Iraqi leader made it clear that he made this humanitarian gesture for Jackson, not for President George Bush.

As was the case seven years before, when he secured the release of Lieutenant Robert Goodman, Jackson returned home to a mixed reaction. President Bush did not seem grateful, and newspaper editorials suggested that Jackson's motives were selfish rather than patriotic. Overshadowed by the growing crisis in the Persian Gulf, the hostage release received little publicity. As biographer Marshall Frady notes,

> What may well have amounted to the most remarkable feat Jackson had pulled off in his entire career had registered in the general mind only flickeringly, and tackily at

Jesse Jackson looks on as a group of former hostages descend the steps of an Iraqi Airways jumbo jet. Jackson helped secure the release of more than three hundred Westerners after the Iraqi invasion of Kuwait in 1990.

that. And then disappeared with virtually no trace, no memory.[108]

Run, Jesse, Run?

In 1991, more than a year before the next presidential election, polls showed Jackson leading the other major contender for the Democratic nomination, New York governor Mario Cuomo, by ten points. Most people expected Jackson to run again, but Democratic officials feared that another race by Jackson might divide the party in the primaries and make it more difficult to win the general election. Once again, party officials adopted primary election rules that made it difficult for a candidate like Jackson to win many delegates.

In November 1991 Jackson announced that he would not be a candidate for president in 1992. Jackson's decision opened the door for another candidate to capture the southern states that had been Jackson's domain for two elections. The Democrat who was able to take advantage of the opening was Arkansas governor Bill Clinton. He won most of the southern primaries, helping earn him the presidential nomination.

Jackson thought he might receive the vice presidential nomination, but Clinton did not select him. Knowing that traditional, liberal Democratic candidates had lost three straight presidential elections, Clinton tried to portray himself as a "new," moderate Democrat. Having Jackson as the vice presidential nominee would make it easy for the Republicans to brand the Democratic ticket as liberal.

Clinton surprised Jackson at a Rainbow Coalition conference in Washington held shortly before the Democratic National Convention. While hoping to gain the support of Jackson's followers, Clinton also wanted to make it clear to mainstream voters that he differed from Jackson in many ways. To illustrate this point, Clinton criticized the popular rap performer Sister Souljah, who had advocated killing white people. Clinton also attacked Jackson for not criticizing Souljah's comments. Although Jackson was enraged by Clinton's remarks, he agreed to campaign for the Democratic ticket a fourth time. When asked why he was willing to support Clinton after enduring his criticisms, Jackson told reporters that the issue was not him versus Clinton, but instead Clinton versus George Bush.

Jackson drew large crowds, but the enthusiasm that had been present in 1980, 1984, and 1988 was missing. Largely because third-party candidate Ross Perot drained votes away from Bush, Clinton won the election. Jackson hoped that he would be repaid for his loyalty to the party by being named ambassador to the United Nations, but that did not happen.

Returning from church services with Jesse Jackson, President-elect Bill Clinton waves to reporters outside the Governor's mansion in Little Rock, Arkansas, in November 1992.

Not being part of the Clinton administration did not diminish Jackson's popularity. In fact, talk grew that he should again run for president—this time as a third-party candidate. A 1994 poll showed that 86 percent of black Americans regarded Jackson as their most important leader. Looking ahead to 1996, blacks favored him by 10 percent over Clinton and by 40 percent over General Colin Powell, the former head of the Joint Chiefs of Staff. Jackson knew that if he ran as an independent in 1996, he would draw enough votes from President Clinton to hand the election to the Republicans. He did not want to do that, so he declined to run.

At the same time, Clinton finally reached out to Jackson. After one of Jackson's trips to the Middle East, the president asked him to come to the White House and describe what he had seen and heard. Clinton also asked Jackson to head the official U.S. delegation monitoring the first South African elections held after the racial policy of apartheid.

A New Organization

With less time to devote to the two organizations he had founded, Operation PUSH and the Rainbow Coalition, Jackson decided to merge the two. In September 1996 Jackson announced the formation of a new organization called the Rainbow/PUSH Coalition. Jackson pledged to continue both groups' missions of promoting peace, civil rights, and economic and social justice across race, class, and gender lines. Jackson hoped that as president of the new Rainbow/PUSH Coalition he would have a stronger platform than ever for speaking out against injustice.

Jackson's decades-long fight for social justice made him one of the most highly respected persons in the nation. He was ranked on the Gallup List of the Ten Most Respected Americans for ten straight years. He also received honorary degrees from more than forty colleges and universities.

Despite the awards and accolades, Jackson grew restless. He felt that his talents were not being used to their best advantage. According to political writer Stanley Crouch,

A man like this must be used for large tasks. He could be
the one who forges the necessary alliances between
Afro-American communities and the local police; the
one who leads the war against drugs through the people
themselves; the one who might so change the climate in
poor neighborhoods that the goal of law and order becomes an inspiration to active engagement; the one who
could instigate and mediate reform in public schools,
raising them to the position they should have in a democratic society. . . . He must be an empowered activist,
and nothing less.[109]

Without the day-to-day coverage of a political campaign,
Jackson's actions rarely made front-page news. To make sure his

*Jesse Jackson announces an accord in 1997 between the Rainbow/PUSH
Coalition and Mitsubishi Motors on the automobile manufacturer's efforts
to promote diversity in its work force.*

Jesse Jackson meets with President Clinton and U.S. secretary of state Madeleine Albright in May 1999 after returning from Belgrade, Yugoslavia, where he had secured the release of three U.S. soldiers who were captured by Serbian forces.

message continued to be heard, Jackson decided in 1992 to host a CNN television show called *Both Sides with Jesse Jackson.* He also wrote a weekly newspaper column.

"A Citizen of the World"

In the 1990s Jackson began to refer to himself as "a citizen of the world." [110] In the spring of 1994 he was invited by the Israelis and Palestinians, traditional enemies, to come to the Middle East. He carried a message of nonviolence. For six days he relayed messages between Israeli and Palestinian leaders. At one point he asked youths from both sides to join hands and sing the old civil rights anthem "We Shall Overcome."

In 1997 President Clinton and Secretary of State Madeleine Albright named him "Special Envoy for the Promotion of Democracy in Africa." Jackson was extremely pleased with the position. He also continued to make nonpolitical trips abroad.

He visited Armenia after a major earthquake, comforting old women and children who had lost their homes. Despite their devastation, they were inspired by this tall, impressive black American. When Jackson told them, "Keep hope alive!" they responded, "Kep hop aliff!" [111]

The Wall Street Project

As the decade drew to a close, Jackson's travels abroad slowed. Back home, he returned to an earlier theme: the importance of economic power. On January 15, 1997—what would have been Martin Luther King Jr.'s fifty-eighth birthday—the Rainbow/ PUSH Coalition launched the Wall Street Project. The aim was to get businesses to hire and promote more minorities and women as executives and board members, to award more contracts to minority- and woman-led businesses, and to encourage the growing black middle class to invest in the stock market.

In the summer of 1998, Jackson announced to a crowd of three thousand at the National Urban League convention in Philadelphia that the Rainbow/PUSH Coalition was now buying stock in order to have some say in corporate policies. He urged other black organizations to do the same. Jackson believed that encouraging companies to diversify their work forces and spread their investments to minority businesses was the next frontier of the civil rights movement. He no longer used words like *racism* or *discrimination*; now he talked about *inclusion* and *economic power.*

In this battle, Jackson was more of an insider than ever before. He was also more realistic, less angry. In early 1999, to celebrate the second anniversary of the Wall Street Project, Jackson organized a conference in New York City. He persuaded President Clinton, Secretary of the Treasury Robert Rubin, Secretary of Commerce William Daley, and Secretary of Labor Alexis Herman to attend. The *New York Times* described the scene:

> In seminars above the snow clouds at the top of the World Trade Center, on the podium above the neon tickers of the New York Stock Exchange, introducing President Clinton or hobnobbing with Wall Street tycoons

at a black-tie soiree, Mr. Jackson teased, inspired and generally enthralled the crowd. His rolling-thunder speaking style, his witty asides, sprawling metaphors and full-flower alliteration had this button-down collection of businessmen and businesswomen laughing, clapping, chanting approval and spewing scorn.[112]

To show that "we have taken our battle from the picket line to the board room," Jackson announced that the Wall Street Project had bought stock in more than one hundred multinational companies, and would exert economic influence. He used the Boeing Company as an example. Every 747 airplane has 4 million parts, Jackson said. "As part of this struggle, we need to measure progress not just by pilots and flight attendants but also by contracts to supply rivets, pistons, carpets and, yes, peanuts."[113]

Because of Jackson's numerous successes, many experts and many of his supporters expected Jackson to run for president a third time. In the spring of 1999, however, Jackson announced that he would not run for president in 2000. Although his support remained intact, he feared that his entry might have complicated the campaign of the favorite, Vice President Al Gore, who had become a friend during the Clinton administration. Jackson said he wanted to concentrate his energy on economic issues of importance to minorities that are outside of government. "The time spent running for president is time that cannot be spent doing something else,"[114] he said.

Jackson Goes to the Balkans

Just one month after announcing that he would not run for president, Jackson found himself doing the type of thing that he wanted to remain free to do. On May 1, 1999, he led a nineteen-member interfaith delegation to Belgrade, Yugoslavia, to negotiate for the release of three American soldiers who had been held hostage by the Yugoslav government since March 31. The soldiers had been captured while patrolling the border between Kosovo and Macedonia in the first days of the NATO bombing in the Balkans. After Jackson urged NATO to halt further air strikes and open negotiations on the fate of Kosovo, Yugoslav president Slobodan Milosevic released the prisoners.

Although President Clinton and NATO officials hailed the release of the Americans, the bombing continued. As before, Jackson endured criticism as well as praise for his actions. Alex Todorovic, a Belgrade journalist covering the Balkan crisis for the online Salon News, wrote that Jackson had offended many people by meeting and shaking hands with Milosevic, whom many people consider a war criminal. Todorovic also pointed out that Jackson, a religious man, was not sensitive to the beliefs of others he met during the trip. According to Todorovic, Jackson "put former communists and atheists on the spot by asking them to join him in prayer—but neglected to pray when he met with Serbia's religious leader, Patriarch Pavle, instead talking politics." But, the writer admitted, "it was vintage Jackson and, somehow, it worked." [115]

Jackson and the Future

Jesse Jackson does not like to plan his life too carefully. He prefers to take life as it comes and keep himself in a position to act swiftly.

Jesse Jackson and members of the interfaith delegation he led to Yugoslavia pose for photographers with the three American soldiers they freed from a Serbian prison.

A Man of Traditional Values

Though often called a liberal, Jesse Jackson holds some deeply conservative values. Author Marshall Frady quoted him in *Jesse: The Life and Pilgrimage of Jesse Jackson*.

> My values come out of a conservative Christian orientation. Probably surprises a lot of people to know I think that way, but it's what I really believe, deep down in my soul. Way back when liberals were dismissing drugs as just a personal habit, I was already saying it's the number one threat to our national security. When I was arguing that our youth was suffering from lack of discipline and growing decadence in our culture, many liberals, quote-unquote, were wafflin' on those issues.

Jackson also discussed his views on sex.

> [People say], "But Reverend Jackson, the new thing is, sex is a thrill." Le'me tell you, it *always* was. But we [are] not an amoebae or paramecium, we have more than one cell, and we can have more than one thrill. We must broaden the basis of our thrill syndrome. Sex is a thrill, but so is having breakfast in the morning a thrill, graduating is a thrill, going to college is a thrill. Becoming mayor, becoming governor, becoming president, your whole life can be a thrill!

In early 1999 Jesse Jackson wrote a syndicated newspaper column called "The Seeds We've Sown." In this column, Jackson discussed America's prison system.

> A story that the news missed last year will plague us in the future years. Across America, communities have adjusted to a growing jail industrial complex. Two million Americans are in prison. . . . Somehow we have come to accept second-class schools and first-class jails. Politicians posture about making sentences longer, about locking up kids earlier and making jail conditions harsher. . . . Get-tough politicians would rather spend more for jails that are worse. The results are perverse. These jails are colleges of crime. Prisons brutalize and stigmatize more of our population than those of any other modern industrial country. . . . We reap what we sow. The seeds planted in the past year—both the fruitful and the poisonous—we will reap in the years to come—for better and for worse.

Although it is not clear exactly what kind of work he will take on in the first years of the twenty-first century, there is no doubt that he will build on his accomplishments in the last decades of the twentieth century. Roy Wilkins, a veteran civil rights leader and aide to Martin Luther King Jr., called Jackson one of the ten or fifteen most important contributors to the development of America in the 1900s. He inspired entire generations of blacks, as well as other groups, that they could realistically think about becoming president of the United States. Among those who may make a run for the White House is Jackson's own son, Jesse Jackson Jr., a member of the U.S. House of Representatives representing the South Side of Chicago.

In a fitting analogy for the former football star who went on to much greater accomplishments off the field, Roy Wilkins said of Jesse Jackson, "If I were a football team, I'd choose Jackson as my fullback. . . . [He] would get lots and lots of touchdowns because the guy is never going to give up, as long as there's a breath in him. He is a marvel." [116]

For years, Jesse Jackson has loved to hear the roar of crowds. He heard his first cheers on the football field in his segregated hometown of Greenville, South Carolina. As a young man in North Carolina and Chicago, the cheers followed his civil rights speeches and sermons. In 1984 crowds around the country yelled, "Run, Jesse, run!" In 1988 they roared, "Win, Jesse, win!"

Jesse Jackson ran for president twice but never won. However, as the influential black magazine *Ebony* once wrote, Jackson did not have to win an election to be a winner:

> When other candidates talk about funding the African National Congress, Jesse's winning. When a poor and fatherless teenage boy in Jackson, Miss. says he knows he can be somebody because Jesse told him just because he was born in the slum doesn't mean the slum was born in him, Jesse's winning. When white farmers, black laborers, senior citizens and jobless youth stand together from Massachusetts to Memphis to Maine to Mississippi in a bold attempt to change the course of American history, Jesse's winning. . . . The real question is not "How can Jesse win?" The real question is "How can Jesse lose?" [117]

Jesse Jackson remains a powerful advocate of human rights and social change.

The answer to that question, of course, is that Jesse Jackson cannot lose. His entire life has been a victory over crushingly difficult circumstances and seemingly insurmountable obstacles. The world today is very different from the one into which Jackson was born in 1941. Greater opportunities exist for all Americans today than ever before—in part because of the untiring efforts and unbreakable spirit of Jesse Louis Jackson.

Notes

Introduction: The Orator

1. Interview with Bradley Steffens, July 1999.

Chapter 1: Greenville, South Carolina

2. Quoted in *Frontline*, "The Pilgrimage of Jesse Jackson," 1996. www2.pbs.org/wgbh/pages/frontline/jesse/.
3. Quoted in Marshall Frady, *Jesse: The Life and Pilgrimage of Jesse Jackson.* New York: Random House, 1996, p. 151.
4. Quoted in Barbara A. Reynolds, *Jesse Jackson: The Man, the Movement, the Myth.* Chicago: Nelson-Hall, 1975, p. 21.
5. Quoted in Frady, *Jesse,* p. 86.
6. Quoted in Frady, *Jesse,* pp. 86–87.
7. Quoted in Reynolds, *Jesse Jackson,* p. 23.
8. Quoted in Frady, *Jesse,* p. 87.
9. Quoted in Reynolds, *Jesse Jackson,* p. 28.
10. Quoted in Frady, *Jesse,* p. 101.
11. Quoted in Frady, *Jesse,* p. 114.
12. Quoted in Frady, *Jesse,* p. 114.
13. Quoted in Frady, *Jesse,* p. 89.
14. Quoted in Frady, *Jesse,* p. 89.
15. Quoted in Frady, *Jesse,* p. 89.
16. Quoted in Frady, *Jesse,* p. 89.
17. Quoted in Frady, *Jesse,* p. 90.
18. Quoted in Frady, *Jesse,* p. 98.
19. Quoted in Frady, *Jesse,* pp. 98–99.
20. Quoted in Frady, *Jesse,* p. 105.
21. Quoted in Reynolds, *Jesse Jackson,* p. 33.
22. Quoted in Barbara A. Reynolds, *Jesse Jackson: America's*

David. Washington, DC: JFJ Associates, 1986, p. 34.

23. Quoted in Frady, *Jesse,* pp. 137–38.

Chapter 2: The Call

24. Quoted in Frady, *Jesse,* p. 130.
25. Quoted in Frady, *Jesse,* p. 130.
26. Quoted in Frady, *Jesse,* p. 139.
27. Quoted in Frady, *Jesse,* pp. 139–40.
28. Quoted in Frady, *Jesse,* p. 131.
29. Quoted in Frady, *Jesse,* p. 134.
30. Quoted in Frady, *Jesse,* p. 135.
31. Quoted in Frady, *Jesse,* p. 170.
32. Quoted in Eddie Stone, *Jesse Jackson.* Los Angeles: Holloway House, 1984, p. 166.
33. Quoted in Frady, *Jesse,* p. 151.
34. Quoted in Frady, *Jesse,* p. 147.
35. Quoted in Frady, *Jesse,* p. 172.
36. Quoted in Frady, *Jesse,* p. 173.
37. Quoted in Frady, *Jesse,* p. 116.
38. Quoted in Reynolds, *Jesse Jackson,* pp. 39–40.
39. Quoted in Reynolds, *Jesse Jackson,* p. 39.
40. Quoted in Reynolds, *Jesse Jackson,* p. 40.
41. Quoted in Frady, *Jesse,* pp. 183–84.
42. Quoted in Frady, *Jesse,* p. 185.
43. Quoted in Frady, *Jesse,* p. 184.

Chapter 3: The Martin Luther King Jr. Years

44. Quoted in Frady, *Jesse,* p. 191.
45. Quoted in Frady, *Jesse,* pp. 191–92.
46. Quoted in Frady, *Jesse,* p. 193.
47. Quoted in Frady, *Jesse,* p. 194.
48. Quoted in Frady, *Jesse,* p. 205.
49. Quoted in Frady, *Jesse,* p. 205.
50. Quoted in Frady, *Jesse,* p. 207.
51. Quoted in Frady, *Jesse,* pp. 224–25.
52. Quoted in Frady, *Jesse,* p. 225.
53. Quoted in Frady, *Jesse,* p. 226.
54. Quoted in Frady, *Jesse,* p. 227.

55. Quoted in Frady, *Jesse*, p. 227.

Chapter 4: "I Am Somebody"

56. Quoted in *Frontline*, "The Pilgrimage of Jesse Jackson."
57. Quoted in Frady, *Jesse*, p. 233.
58. Quoted in Frady, *Jesse*, p. 233.
59. Quoted in Frady, *Jesse*, p. 229.
60. Quoted in Reynolds, *Jesse Jackson*, p. 83.
61. Quoted in *Frontline*, "The Pilgrimage of Jesse Jackson."
62. Quoted in Reynolds, *Jesse Jackson*, p. 83.
63. Quoted in Frady, *Jesse*, p. 234.
64. Quoted in Frady, *Jesse*, p. 230.
65. Quoted in Frady, *Jesse*, p. 243.
66. Quoted in Frady, *Jesse*, p. 244.
67. Quoted in Frady, *Jesse*, p. 247.
68. Quoted in Frady, *Jesse*, p. 271.
69. Quoted in *Frontline*, "The Pilgrimage of Jesse Jackson."
70. Quoted in Stone, *Jesse Jackson*, pp. 155–56.
71. Quoted in Frady, *Jesse*, p. 290.
72. Quoted in Stone, *Jesse Jackson*, p. 137.
73. Quoted in Stone, *Jesse Jackson*, p. 138.
74. Quoted in Frady, *Jesse*, p. 291.
75. Quoted in Stone, *Jesse Jackson*, p. 143.

Chapter 5: The First Presidential Campaign

76. Quoted in Reynolds, *Jesse Jackson*, p. 28.
77. Quoted in Frady, *Jesse*, p. 169.
78. Quoted in Stone, *Jesse Jackson*, p. 191.
79. Quoted in Frady, *Jesse*, p. 306.
80. Quoted in Bob Faw and Nancy Skelton, *Thunder in America*. Austin: Texas Monthly, 1986, pp. 98–99.
81. Quoted in Frady, *Jesse*, p. 339.
82. Quoted in Stone, *Jesse Jackson*, p. 159.
83. Quoted in Frady, *Jesse*, p. 343.
84. Quoted in Frady, *Jesse*, p. 350.
85. Quoted in Frady, *Jesse*, p. 14.
86. Quoted in Tom Morgenthau, "What Jesse Jackson Wants," *Newsweek*, May 7, 1984, p. 41.

87. Quoted in *Frontline*, "The Pilgrimage of Jesse Jackson."
88. Quoted in *Frontline*, "The Pilgrimage of Jesse Jackson."
89. Quoted in *Frontline*, "The Pilgrimage of Jesse Jackson."
90. Quoted in *Frontline*, "The Pilgrimage of Jesse Jackson."
91. Quoted in Frady, *Jesse*, p. 376.
92. Quoted in Frady, *Jesse*, p. 368.

Chapter 6: A Second Try

93. Howard Fineman, "Jackson's New Clout," *Newsweek*, December 14, 1987, p. 50.
94. Laura B. Randolph, "Can Jesse Jackson Win?" *Ebony*, March 1988, p. 161.
95. Quoted in Joe Klein, "Jesse Jackson for *President?*" *New York Times*, April 11, 1988, p. 22.
96. Quoted in Klein, "Jesse Jackson for *President?*" p. 23.
97. Quoted in Frady, *Jesse*, p. 393.
98. Quoted in Frady, *Jesse*, p. 396.
99. Stanley Crouch, "Beyond Good and Evil," *New Republic*, June 20, 1988, p. 22.
100. Quoted in Frady, *Jesse*, p. 396.
101. Quoted in Frady, *Jesse*, p. 398.
102. Quoted in Frady, *Jesse*, p. 408.
103. Quoted in Frady, *Jesse*, p. 409.
104. Quoted in Jacob V. Lamar, "Reaching Common Ground," *Time*, August 1, 1988, p. 18.
105. Quoted in *Frontline*, "The Pilgrimage of Jesse Jackson."
106. Quoted in Lamar, "Reaching Common Ground," p. 19.
107. Quoted in Crouch, "Beyond Good and Evil," pp. 15–16.

Chapter 7: "A Citizen of the World"

108. Quoted in Frady, *Jesse*, p. 540.
109. Quoted in Crouch, "Beyond Good and Evil," p. 23.
110. Quoted in Frady, *Jesse*, p. 426.
111. Quoted in Frady, *Jesse*, pp. 20–21.
112. Joseph Kahn, "Jackson Challenges 'Capital of Capital,'" *New York Times*, January 16, 1999, p. C3.
113. Quoted in Kahn, "Jackson Challenges 'Capital of Capital,'" p. C3.

114. Quoted in *New York Times*, "Jackson Says He'll Focus on His Corporate Project," March 25, 1999, p. A16.

115. Alex Todorovic, "Winning Ugly," Salon News, May 3, 1999. www.salon.com/news/feature/1999/05/03/jackson/index.html.

116. Quoted in *Frontline*, "The Pilgrimage of Jesse Jackson."

117. Quoted in Randolph, "Can Jesse Jackson Win?" p. 162.

Important Dates in the Life of Jesse Jackson

1941

Jesse Louis Burns is born.

1944

Jackson's mother, Helen, marries Charles Jackson.

1947

Jackson gets his first job helping deliver stove wood in a pickup truck.

1949

Jackson whistles at a white grocery store clerk for service; the man pulls a gun on Jackson and berates him.

1957

Charles Jackson legally adopts Jesse; Jesse takes the last name "Jackson."

1959

Jackson graduates from Sterling High School in Greenville, South Carolina, and, after turning down a contract to play professional baseball, enrolls at the University of Illinois.

1960

Jackson transfers to North Carolina Agricultural & Technical College (A&T) in Greensboro, North Carolina.

1962

Jackson marries Jacqueline "Jackie" Lavinia Brown.

1963

Jackson helps lead civil rights demonstrations in Greensboro; that spring, he graduates from North Carolina A&T.

1964

Jackson enters the Chicago Theological Seminary.

1965

Jackson heads south to Selma, Alabama, to take part in civil rights protests; he meets Martin Luther King Jr. and asks for a job.

1966

Jackson becomes head of the Chicago chapter of the Southern Christian Leadership Conference's economic arm, Operation Breadbasket; becomes active in that city's civil rights activities.

1967

Jackson is named national director of Operation Breadbasket.

1968

Jackson is at the Lorraine Motel when Martin Luther King Jr. is assassinated in Memphis, Tennessee; Jackson flies back to Chicago that night and appears in public the next day wearing the clothes bearing King's blood; a controversy over exactly how close Jackson was to King begins; a few weeks later, Jackson is the "mayor" of "Resurrection City," the tent encampment in Washington, D.C., that symbolized the Poor People's Campaign.

1971

Jackson organizes the first Black Expo; he later resigns from the Southern Christian Leadership Conference and starts Operation PUSH.

1972

Jackson becomes an activist at the Democratic National Convention in Miami Beach.

1977

Jackson organizes Operation PUSH-Excel, an educational program for inner-city youngsters.

1979

Jackson makes a controversial visit to the Middle East.

1983

Jackson enters the 1984 presidential race; in December, he makes a controversial trip to Syria to help free navy pilot Robert Goodman, who was being held hostage.

1984

Jackson's presidential campaign stumbles after he makes a disparaging remark about the Jewish population of New York City; despite several strong primary showings, he loses to former vice president Walter Mondale; Jackson makes an inspiring speech at the convention in San Francisco, then campaigns hard for Mondale in the fall.

1987

Jackson decides to run again for the presidency.

1988

His second race is even more successful than the first, but once again Jackson loses, this time to Massachusetts governor Michael Dukakis; Jackson gives a stirring speech at the Democratic National Convention in Atlanta and works hard for the Democratic ticket in the fall.

1991

Jackson travels to the Middle East and secures the release of hundreds of hostages being held by Saddam Hussein; he decides against running for president in 1992.

1996

Jackson's Rainbow Coalition and Operation PUSH merge to form the Rainbow/PUSH Coalition.

1997

President Bill Clinton and Secretary of State Madeleine Albright appoint Jackson special envoy to Africa; Jackson also launches the Wall Street Project to focus attention on the economic issues of minorities.

1999

President Clinton and other dignitaries speak at the second anniversary conference of the Wall Street Project; Jackson announces he will not run for president in 2000; he helps free three American servicemen captured by Yugoslavia; he is arrested while protesting the zero-tolerance policies of Eisenhower High School in Decatur, Illinois, that led to the expulsion of six African-American students.

For Further Reading

Ralph David Abernathy, *And the Walls Came Tumbling Down.* New York: Harper and Row, 1989. A memoir by one of Martin Luther King Jr.'s closest aides.

Taylor Branch, *Parting the Waters: America in the King Years, 1954–63.* New York: Simon and Schuster, 1988. A well-written look at the early years of the civil rights movement.

David J. Garrow, *Bearing the Cross: Martin Luther King Jr. and the Southern Christian Leadership Conference.* New York: William Morrow, 1986. A scholarly look at the civil rights organization with which Jesse Jackson began his career.

Peter Goldman, Tom Matthews, and the Newsweek Special Election Team, *Quest for the Presidency: The 1988 Campaign.* New York: Touchstone/Simon and Schuster, 1989. A comprehensive look back at the 1988 presidential race.

Coretta Scott King, *My Life with Martin Luther King Jr.* New York: Holt, Rinehart, and Winston, 1969. A memoir by King's widow.

Kevin Phillips, *The Politics of Rich and Poor.* New York: Random House, 1990. An analysis of the politics of poverty.

Internet Sources

AfricaNews Online (www.AfricaNews.org). AfricaNews covers Jackson well through its news bureau.

Rainbow/PUSH Coalition (www.rainbowpush.org). The Rainbow/PUSH Coalition website offers up-to-date information on the organization, with a great deal of admiring information about Jesse Jackson.

Works Consulted

Books

Lerone Bennett Jr., *The Shaping of Black America*. Chicago: Johnson, 1975. A history of blacks in this country since the first twenty landed at Jamestown in 1619.

Editors of Time-Life Books, *African Americans: Voices of Triumph*. Alexandria, VA: Time-Life Books, 1993. A well-illustrated, wide-ranging look at black Americans.

Bob Faw and Nancy Skelton, *Thunder in America*. Austin: Texas Monthly, 1986. A very detailed and fair book about "the improbable [1984] presidential campaign of Jesse Jackson," by two reporters who covered it.

Marshall Frady, *Jesse: The Life and Pilgrimage of Jesse Jackson*. New York: Random House, 1996. This exhaustive "political biography" explores the many facets of Jackson's character, at the same time providing a perceptive examination of race relations in America. Frady draws on hundreds of sources in what is generally regarded as the most complete picture of this complex character.

Langston Hughes, Milton Meltzer, and C. Eric Lincoln, *A Pictorial History of Black Americans*. New York: Crown, 1973. This book contains over twelve hundred illustrations and historical text; considered a classic work.

Florence Jackson, *Blacks in America, 1954–1979*. New York: Franklin Watts, 1980. A concise illustrated history of blacks in the United States.

Jesse L. Jackson, *Straight from the Heart*. Philadelphia: Fortress, 1987. Jesse Jackson's first book is a collage of thirty-six public speeches, sermons, eulogies, essays, and interviews on topics ranging from politics and human rights to religion, education, and business.

Thomas Landess and Richard Quinn, *Jesse Jackson and the Politics of Race*. Ottawa, IL: Jameson Books, 1985. A book that combines an objective analysis of Jackson's rise with the overall civil rights movement in America.

Adolph L. Reed Jr., *The Jesse Jackson Phenomenon: The Crisis of Purpose in Afro-American Politics*. New Haven, CT: Yale University Press, 1987. A scholarly analysis of Jackson, black Americans, and contemporary politics.

Barbara A. Reynolds, *Jesse Jackson: America's David*. Washington, DC: JFJ Associates, 1985. Originally published in 1975 as *Jesse Jackson: The Man, the Movement, the Myth*, this is a fair, although now somewhat dated, portrait of a man the author sees as a "David" fighting the modern-day Goliath of bigotry and intolerance.

Eddie Stone, *Jesse Jackson*. Los Angeles: Holloway House, 1984. An easy-to-read and very admiring look at Jackson, but filled with significant factual errors.

Periodicals

Jonathan Alter, "Jackson's Message," *Newsweek*, March 21, 1988. A fair examination of whether Jackson is really addressing the issues in the presidential race.

Fred Barnes, "Jesse Goes Country," *New Republic*, August 3, 1987. A long magazine piece detailing Jackson's search for the mainstream Democratic vote.

William F. Buckley, "Liberals and the Jackson Race," *National Review*, December 9, 1983. A conservative view of what Jackson's presidential campaign might mean.

Nancy Cooper, "Keeping His Eyes on the Next Prize," *Newsweek*, November 21, 1988. Asks, but does not answer: Where does Jackson go from here?

Stanley Crouch, "Beyond Good and Evil," *New Republic,* June 20, 1988. The paradoxes of Jesse Jackson.

Howard Fineman, "Jackson's New Clout," *Newsweek*, December 14, 1987. A look at Jackson's possible role as "kingmaker."

Diana B. Henriques, "Project for Minorities Aims to Show Its Broader Mandate," *New York Times*, January 14, 1999. Preview of the Wall Street Project conference.

Hendrik Hertzberg, "Jesse Is History," *New Republic*, June 20, 1988. The author discusses Jackson in terms of his history-making life.

Jesse Jackson, "High Crimes and Misdemeanors," *Los Angeles Times*, December 20, 1998. Comments on the eve of President Clinton's impeachment.

———, "The Seeds We've Sown," *Los Angeles Times*, January 3, 1999. Comments about the upcoming year.

———, "We Are Searching for a Leader," *U.S. News & World Report*, November 26, 1984. Comments after the 1984 election.

Hamilton Jordan, "A Black Candidate in '84?" *Newsweek*, June 20, 1983. Former president Carter's chief of staff assesses the possible impact of Jackson's candidacy.

Joseph Kahn, "Jackson Challenges 'Capital of Capital,'" *New York Times*, January 16, 1999. A glowing piece on the second annual Wall Street Project meeting.

Joe Klein, "Jesse Jackson for *President?*" *New York Times*, April 11, 1988. A very negative piece shortly before the New York primary.

Morton M. Kondracke, "Endless Quest," *New Republic*, August 8 and 15, 1988. What is next for Jackson?

Peter B. Kovler, "Jackson's Candidacy: Tiptoeing Around the Questions," *Commonweal*, April 8, 1988. An article wondering whether Jackson is "the right pioneer."

Michael Kramer, "The Jackson Problem," *Time*, December 12, 1988. A perceptive piece on the problems he will have holding on to his role as the number-one black leader.

Jacob V. Lamar, "Reaching Common Ground," *Time*, August 1, 1988. An in-depth postconvention story of how Michael Dukakis managed to get Jackson (publicly at least) to join the team.

Larry Martz, "Jackson's Big Takeoff," *Newsweek*, April 11, 1988. A midcampaign story.

————, "The Power Broker," *Newsweek*, March 21, 1988. Another midcampaign story.

Marci McDonald, "The Jackson Factor," *Maclean's*, April 11, 1988. The view from Canada, mid-1988 campaign.

John McLaughlin, "Jackson the Moderate," *National Review*, July 17, 1987. A conservative look at Jackson's campaign.

Jason Method, "Jesse Jackson Takes Case to Corporate Board-rooms," *Asbury Park*, (New Jersey) *Press*, August 6, 1988. A report on Jackson's address to the National Urban League convention.

Tom Morgenthau, "A Black Candidate in 1984?" *Newsweek*, June 6, 1983. Another early piece looking ahead to Jackson's campaign.

————, "What Jesse Jackson Wants," *Newsweek*, May 7, 1984. A midcampaign look at Jackson's campaign.

————, "What Makes Jesse Run?" *Newsweek*, November 14, 1983. A long analytical piece that sums up Jackson's presidential race.

Salim Muwakkil, "Jackson's Challenge," *Progressive*, July 1987. An argument that Jackson must be more radical, not less, in order to win.

National Review, "The Democrats' Tar Baby," April 29, 1988. An anti-Jackson piece suggesting he appeals only to blacks and "a tiny sliver" of whites.

————, "The Front Runner," July 3, 1987. A look at the Jesse Jackson phenomenon.

————, "Reflections on Jackson," November 25, 1983. A negative assessment of Jackson's presidential chances.

New York Times, "Jackson Says He'll Focus on His Corporate Project," March 25, 1999. Brief story on Jackson passing up the 2000 presidential race.

David North, "Jesse Jackson's Flawed Crusade," *Maclean's*, July 23, 1984. A Canadian magazine's perspective on Jackson's campaign.

Laura B. Randolph, "Can Jesse Jackson Win?" *Ebony*, March 1988. A very laudatory piece in a major black magazine.

Richard Stengel, "An Indelicate Balance," *Time*, July 25, 1988. Postconvention coverage.

Sol Stern, "Jesse's Jews," *New Republic*, June 20, 1988. Jackson's problem with Jewish voters is worse than most people think, the writer says.

Mary Summers, "The Front-Runner," *Nation*, November 28, 1987. A review of four books about Jackson, by his 1984 presidential campaign speechwriter.

Jeannye Thornton with John W. Mashek, "Jesse Jackson Shakes Up Race for White House," *U.S. News & World Report*, December 19, 1983. An analysis of how Jackson's impact could reach beyond the presidential race.

U.S. News & World Report, "For Me There Is a Double Standard," December 21, 1987. Interview with Jackson about Fidel Castro, Yasir Arafat, and his own public image.

————, "Jesse Jackson's White House Bid," November 14, 1983. An early piece about Jackson's first presidential race.

Kenneth T. Walsh with Jeannye Thornton, "Where Hart and Jackson Go from Here," *U.S. News & World Report*, July 23, 1984. An analysis of what happens now that they both lost.

Jacob Weisberg, "The Disorganization Man," *Newsweek*, August 7, 1987. Discusses how PUSH's troubles could hurt the campaign.

Lawrence Zuckerman, "Has He Got a Free Ride?" *Time*, April 18, 1988. A short piece in the middle of the campaign, asking if the press is afraid of Jackson, then saying it has scrutinized him closer than any other candidate.

Internet Sources

Joel Deane, "Jackson to Web-Announce Candidacy," ZDNN Tech News, March 23, 1999. www.zdnet.com/zdnn/stories/news/0,4586,2230579,00.html. A preview of Jackson's announcement the following day concerning the 2000 presidential race.

Frontline, "The Pilgrimage of Jesse Jackson," 1996. www2.pbs. org/wgbh/pages/frontline/jesse/. Material from the *Frontline* television show "The Pilgrimage of Jesse Jackson," which aired in 1996. Includes transcripts of the show, full interviews, and much related information.

Alex Todorovic, "Winning Ugly," Salon News, May 3, 1999. www.salon.com/news/feature/1999/05/03/jackson/index. html. An article that describes Jackson's missteps and gaffes while securing the release of three American servicemen in Yugoslavia but admits "Jesse Jackson gets his men."

Index

Picture Credits

About the Authors

A widely published poet and playwright, Bradley Steffens is the author of fourteen books, including *Free Speech, Censorship,* and *The Importance of Emily Dickinson.* He lives in Poway, California.

Dan Woog is the author of a dozen books and thousands of magazine and newspaper articles. His award-winning column, "Woog's World," appears weekly in Connecticut's *Westport News.* He is also a soccer coach who, in 1990, was named National Youth Coach of the Year. He lives in Westport, Connecticut.